Paul Keith Davis has been entrusted with precious jewels of the treasury of Heaven, bringing revelation about divine mysteries to the Body of Christ. *Books of Destiny* is replete with Scriptures and correlating experiences from dear saints, past and present, and includes some of his own divine encounters. If there was ever a time that we need his wisdom and revelation, it is now!

—JILL AUSTIN
Founder and President, Master Potter Ministries

*Books of Destiny* is a window into understanding key mysteries about the spiritual realm. Paul Keith Davis provides insight that is not just helpful, but essential to understanding God's Kingdom. I had a dream the first day I met Paul Keith Davis, and in it he sat writing in the library room of Heaven accompanied by the scribe angels of eternity. I believe this book came from his experience and will leave an impartation with its readers.

—SHAWN BOLZ
Author of *The Throne Room Company*

Your heart will be captured and inspired by the revelatory dimensions of this marvelous and exciting book. Paul Keith Davis shares how God is drawing each of us to journey behind the veil into His manifest presence. Read these pages and discover the glorious secrets awaiting you.

—BOBBY CONNER
Founder, Eagle's View Ministries

Life's best moments are always characterized by peace, fulfillment, and blessings—an experience treasured only by those who have truly discovered their destiny or purpose. Paul Keith Davis excellently conveys this age-old principle in his profound work, *Books of Destiny*. This powerful book will incite you to walk in the special plans God has designed for you. I highly recommend it!

—DR. KINGSLEY A. FLETCHER
International Speaker, Government Advisor, Author, Pastor

*Books of Destiny* is full of fresh insight and powerful revelation. It's a timely, must-read book.

—RAY HUGHES
Founder, Selah Ministries

*Books of Destiny* provokes us to a higher calling. Paul Keith Davis's glimpses into the treasury rooms of Heaven are fascinating and powerful. Read this book and discover the great gifts from God awaiting you!

—JOHN PAUL JACKSON
Founder, Streams Ministries International

*Books of Destiny* is a deeply profound book that has the potential to "blow you out of the water." Paul Keith Davis writes with a precision of discernment, prophetic integrity, and accuracy. As you read this book you will be challenged to walk in higher and deeper places in God. Read and absorb.

—PATRICIA KING
Founder, Extreme Prophetic

Paul Keith Davis's *Books of Destiny* takes you into a heavenly realm. He brings you into such an intimate place of revelation that you actually feel as if you are seated at the feet of the Father, experiencing His love and wisdom. This is a book of faith for a hungry generation.

—DR. CHUCK D. PIERCE
President, Glory of Zion International Ministries
Vice President, Global Harvest Ministries

What an encouraging book! By opening the books of destiny for us, Paul Keith Davis has deciphered many divine mysteries concerning the end-times. Coupled with revelations entrusted to well-known leaders, he has compiled a book of hope for the Body of Christ. It made me happy to be a Christian!

—ANNA ROUNTREE
Author of *The Heavens Opened* and *The Priestly Bride*

# BOOKS *of* DESTINY:
## SECRETS OF GOD REVEALED

### PAUL KEITH DAVIS

STREAMS PUBLISHING HOUSE
P.O. Box 550, North Sutton, New Hampshire 03260

ISBN: 1-58483-094-8

Creative Director and Managing Editor: Carolyn Blunk
Editors: Jordan Bateman, Dorian Kreindler
Editorial Assistant: Mary Ballotte
Designed by Dan Jamison
Cover by Mike Bailey

Printed in the United States of America.

---

FOR A FREE CATALOG
OF STREAMS BOOKS AND OTHER MATERIALS,
CALL 1-888-441-8080 (USA AND CANADA)
OR 603-927-4224

---

*Lovingly dedicated to*
*Bob Jones.*
*I am honored to call you*
*my spiritual mentor and friend.*

# CONTENTS

# FOREWORD

For some years the Holy Spirit had been whispering to me about a man I would someday meet upon whom the "spirit of wisdom and revelation" would rest.

At a prophetic gathering in Illinois in 2003, I was privileged to be scheduled to minister alongside Bobby Conner and Paul Keith Davis. For some time I had known and greatly appreciated Bobby, and I had heard much from others—as well as bits and pieces from the Lord—concerning Paul Keith Davis, however, I had not yet had the blessing of meeting him personally.

I arrived at the conference late, and I was unable to meet any speakers before my session began. During the worship service, the Lord gave me a clear picture concerning a man I saw sitting in the audience. I watched the Holy Spirit give him an old quill pen, and the voice of the Dove said: "I am giving this man the pen of the ready writer." Later as I ministered I mentioned this word, not knowing who in the natural this person was. As it ended up, the man in the audience that night was in fact Paul Keith Davis.

After reading the tremendous manuscript *Books of Destiny: Secrets of God Revealed*, my heart leapt with joy to see how true the vision of the "pen of the ready writer" was and how accurate those whisperings of the Holy Spirit were. Paul Keith Davis is one of the purest mouthpieces in the prophetic movement I have ever met, or had the privilege of reading.

Within the pages of this book you will find the "teacher of the Scriptures" and the "revelation of the prophet" converged. Rarely do I find this creative yet scholarly blend merged in one vessel. Truly the School of the Word and the School of the Spirit are at work cooperating together in this unique book.

As I read chapter after chapter, I could not put it down. Alongside Rick Joyner's masterpiece *The Final Quest*, Paul Keith

Davis's *Books of Destiny* is the fastest read I have ever done of any book—not because it is "light reading," but rather the understanding contained in this book so captivated my interest that my entire being became engaged as I consumed each page.

Some years ago on Yom Kippur, I dreamt I was given an ornate antique wooden box that had been unopened for years. The next thing I knew I was given a key to this ancient box, and I inserted it in the opening along the front. The lid popped open, and curiously I looked inside the once-sealed box. To my surprise, an old book rested safely inside. Carefully I withdrew the bound parchment. As I held it endearingly, I read the title: *The End-Time Understandings from the Book of Daniel.* "What a priceless treasure!" the voice of my heart exclaimed.

Contained within the pages of *Books of Destiny* are some of the first installments, I believe, of the divine wisdom from the life and writings of the prophet Daniel, who was noted in Scripture as having an "excellent spirit." Read, pray, peruse, and read it over—again and again.

With humility and accuracy, Paul Keith Davis weaves a tapestry of true-to-life stories from the lives of various pioneers: Katherine Kulhman, Pastor Roland Buck, William Branham, Maria Woodworth-Etter, Bob Jones, Wade Taylor, and others. Oh, to learn lessons from these champions of the faith and pass them on to the next generation is my and author Paul Keith Davis' cry!

What I like most about this book, however, is that it does not lift up or exalt any gifted vessel. The pages of this book exalt Jesus the Messiah! They issue an equal-opportunity invitation for each of you to access greater intimacy with God.

Step up a little higher, and get a sharper view of our glorious Lord. Take and eat. *Books of Destiny* will whet your appetite for a more passionate pursuit of the Lord Himself and His end-time purposes. A feast is set before you!

—JAMES W. GOLL
Cofounder, Encounters Network

# INTRODUCTION

In the aspirations of Heaven, timing is everything. The Father has appointed moments for divine destiny to be fulfilled. Times, seasons, and epochs are a vital component in God's redemptive plan. At the precisely ordained mark, our Redeemer came to earth and, at the assigned hour, the Holy Spirit fell upon the early apostles.

This eternal truth has amplified implications as we approach a pivotal crossroads in Heaven's orchestration of earthly events: God is going to fulfill His grand design. Our Father is determined to find vessels to use in profound and historic ways to glorify His Son. These vessels will be children of destiny who perform the prophetic mandates of a chosen generation. The question remains: Who from among the "called-out ones" will surrender to heavenly objectives and fully submit to God's plans, purposes, and intent?

Throughout the Bible, the Father established specific *kairos* moments and historical periods to accomplish the blueprint of Heaven:

> It is not for you to know times or epochs which the Father has fixed by His own authority.
> —Acts 1:7

Specific appointments with destiny have been determined and reserved by the Father; these moments are established by God's choice and authority. Humanity has not been given exact knowledge of when the fullness of these times and seasons will occur. Nevertheless, with the help of the Holy Spirit, we can discern critical junctures with heavenly destinies. The signs in the Heavens and the prophetic promises of Scripture highlight coming days when we will see a divine fulfillment of God's plans and a harvest of souls.

According to Ephesians 1:10, the Lord has made provision for the maturity of these times; the climax of the ages will bring unity between Heaven and earth. This unity will be accomplished when the Head, the Lord Jesus, is joined to His Body, the Church. This reality will identify the consummation of the ages ordained for a promised generation and the legacy bestowed to the bride of Christ.

## An Appointed Deliverer

Even before Israel was forced to endure the harsh oppression of Egyptian bondage, a divine promise was given to their patriarch, Abraham. He was assured by God that a day of deliverance would come. This promise was an infallible pledge given to a righteous servant with the validation and authenticity of Heaven. It could not fail. To fulfill this divine promise, someone had to be raised up. There was an appointment with destiny for a deliverer to lead Israel to freedom gleaning the wealth of the nation that had enslaved them.

In Moses, the Lord found the man that He would use to bring salvation and deliverance to His people. The time had come for the accomplishment of the prophetic commission for that portion of Israel's history. So it is in this day. Profound promises and mandates are poised to become reality. Each will be as significant in their implications as the Jews' deliverance from the enslavement of Egypt.

God chooses humanity to perform His plan on the earth. That is the model He established with ancient Israel and uses to this day:

We give thanks to You, O God, we give thanks,
For your name is near;
Men declare Your wondrous works.
"When I select an appointed time,
It is I who judge with equity.
The earth and all who dwell in it melt;
It is I who have firmly set its pillars. Selah.
I said to the boastful, 'Do not boast,'
And to the wicked, 'Do not lift up the horn;
Do not lift up your horn on high,
Do not speak with insolent pride.'"
For not from the east, nor from the west,
Nor from the desert comes exaltation;
But God is the Judge;
He puts down one and exalts another.

—Psalm 75:1–7

Almighty God selects and appoints specific times to render justice on the earth. It is by His design that His wondrous acts are performed through vessels of His choice. God humbles one and exalts another.

During designated epochs of spiritual outpouring and diverse expressions of revival, people are apprehended by the Holy Spirit to fulfill their purpose and destiny by God. Notable changes are made in people and circumstances when corporate and personal promises begin to form a living reality. Seeds of destiny are watered by the Spirit and produce a consecrated existence and fruitfulness.

Medical science has proved that many people suffer physical ailments because they perceive a lack of purpose and destiny in their lives. Their reality seems to be empty and meaningless, a perception that results in emotional and bodily weakness.

The good news is that God has an incredible design and dream for every human being. Awareness of His thoughts and aspirations for us births energy and a supernatural invigoration, and awakens us to the fundamental mandate given to humanity in the Garden of Eden. The plans that He has for us are for our welfare and not our calamity. He gives us a future and a hope (Jeremiah 29:11).

The need to have individual purpose and fulfill an ordained task is an underlying part of our human nature. We as humans are designed to exercise our dominion in the earth and be fruitful and multiply. That blessing is imparted to us through the El Shaddai attributes of God. We feel empty when we are not fulfilling that commission.

When we accept the privilege of laboring with Heaven and fulfilling tasks having eternal consequences, we receive a tremendous surge of spiritual energy and a fruit-producing sense of personal duty.

Nevertheless, we need to understand that accomplishing our destiny is not automatic. Decisions and choices must be made; we must be conformed to the plan of Heaven to be led into authority and productivity. We must master valuable lessons to cooperate quickly and easily with Heaven. Once we have learned to be disciples, our diligent prayer should be to remain fully focused on God's objectives and principles.

## Sons and Daughters of Destiny

Several years ago, a woman named Kathryn Kuhlman emerged from obscurity to provide a bridge that carried the Church from the revival of the 1940s and '50s to today. She had a very powerful ministry, demonstrating the Lord's grace and awesomeness during a wilderness season of the Church following the notable healing expression of 1946–1956. Thousands of people were healed and delivered by the Lord through her ministry.

The aptly named biography *Daughter of Destiny* was one of many works to chronicle Kuhlman's life. In the book, author Jamie Buckingham outlined key secrets Kuhlman used to fulfill her appointed destiny at a pivotal time in Church history. She exemplified a coming generation of warriors who will consummate a heavenly commission at this crossroads in human history.

Although her miracle ministry began in the late 1940s, Kuhlman's greatest impact was furnishing a much-needed spiritual rejuvenation during the late '60s and '70s. Eventually, she gained prominent national and international attention and helped carry the Church through to the next phase of God's plan. Her fulfillment of a specific destiny provided a prophetic model for our generation to emulate. She was a fully yielded vessel in the hands of the Lord and was used mightily to accomplish His heavenly directives.

## Friendship with God

One of the primary characteristics of this animated woman's ministry was her intimate relationship with the Holy Spirit. She often called the Holy Spirit her "best friend." Her greatest aspiration was to hold a miracle service, attended by thousands, where every person in the assembly left completely healed and delivered.

The anointing of God resting upon her gave her access to the revelatory realm of Heaven; she was able to give words of knowledge about specific illnesses, individual circumstances, and other information that she had no way of knowing by natural means. This manifestation elevated the faith of the people present, allowing for an even greater flow of miracles.

Her meetings were marked by the tangible presence of God; astounding demonstrations of healing, miracles, and manifestations of power occurred.

Kuhlman often made the statement that she was not the Lord's first choice for the powerful ministry she carried. She believed she was perhaps the Lord's third or fourth alternate for this prominent release of His majesty. According to her testimony, she believed several men declined this opportunity before she yielded her will to that of the Father's.

It seemed the Lord was determined to find someone through whom He could heal the sick and manifest the Kingdom of Heaven. The only question was who that person would be.

## Yielding Our Human Will

One Saturday afternoon, Kathryn Kuhlman made a decision to give herself fully to the plans and purposes of God. That decision launched her into a rich dimension of intimacy with the Lord. As she put it, she "yielded [her] will to the will of the Father."

This surrender fully enthroned the Lord in her spirit, soul, and body. Through her, the Lord began to demonstrate His Kingdom in significant and profound ways. She became a "Kingdom person," tasting the revelatory truth of God and the powers of the Kingdom age (Hebrews 6:5).

A similar opportunity is being given in this strategic hour to God's people. We can fully yield ourselves and walk with Him in the same way pioneers such as Kathryn Kuhlman, John G. Lake, William Branham, and various others have done. This is how "deliverers" are birthed to meet the needs of their generation.

Today, the eyes of the Lord are roving to and fro throughout the earth to find hearts that are completely His. When these sold-out ones are found, Heaven's full support will be placed behind them.

Throughout history one common denominator has been apparent in the Lord's choices for leadership. He chooses the common and ordinary in order to confound the wise. Kathryn Kuhlman was an individual on whom the Lord's favor rested. Throughout her messages, she continually acknowledged that she was an ordinary person with an extraordinary anointing. That is still the Lord's approach—to use the common and mundane to do extravagant and supernatural exploits. God used her in astonishing ways to achieve tremendous miracles.

Kuhlman carried in her heart the dream that someday every church would witness the miracle-working power of God. She wasn't allowed to see that vision fulfilled in her lifetime, though. Nevertheless, she did introduce the Lord Jesus as a living reality before passing into the cloud of witnesses. She completed her assignment and introduced a hungry generation to a captivating relationship with the Holy Spirit.

She had demonstrated to her generation that healing, deliverance, and miracles are the heritage of people who walk with God in harmony and union. Despite her personal failures and shortcomings, she exemplified how God can take imperfect individuals and use them as instruments to reflect His glory and power.

Kuhlman is simply one example of a life used by the Holy Spirit to accomplish a specific purpose and mandate at a specific time in Church history. As the days of destiny unfold before us, we will witness many such encounters with God. Commissions are being granted for ordinary people to live in the reality of a tangible and meaningful relationship with an awesome God. Their conviction will be a defining quality of His end-time army. Invitations and opportunities are being extended in this *kairos* moment of time. Who will respond with yielded hearts?

During a conference in Syracuse, New York, my wife, Wanda, and I were given a picture by a thoughtful woman named Sheila Miller. The picture had a prophetic poem inscribed on it:

*REVELATION* by Sheila Miller

Light released from the Throne,
Swirling, vibrating, and pulsating
with the hidden thoughts of the Creator of Life.
"Let there be Light!" He declares.
His light pierces my soul,
Penetrates my spirit,
and turns darkness into light,
revealing ancient mysteries
for such a time as this!

Presently we are at the threshold of a "fullness of time" juncture in Church history. A door stands open before us, and a Voice calls us to higher, heavenly realms. God invites us to understand experientially the unfolding of heavenly blueprints and to apprehend spiritual mysteries that have been hidden until now. These secrets of God and mysteries of His Kingdom are hidden in the depths of Christ.

PART

I

# BOOKS *of* HEAVEN

# CROSSROADS *of* DESTINY

# 1

# TREASURES
# HIDDEN *in* CHRIST

The library rooms of Heaven are incredible places—palatial rooms filled with books, scrolls, and journals containing precious mysteries, unfathomable knowledge, and boundless wisdom. Visions, revelations, and divine encounters are being given today by God's grace for some to access and articulate the riches contained in these archives of Heaven.

These heavenly manuscripts and parchments provide such a wealth of insight and divine wisdom that it is impossible to assign even one of them a monetary value. The apostle Paul saw these treasures that are hidden in Christ and spoke their words of encouragement to the church of Colossae and to us. He hoped:

> That their hearts may be encouraged, having been knit together in love, and attaining to all the wealth that comes from the full assurance of understanding,

resulting in a true knowledge of God's mystery, that is, Christ Himself, in whom are hidden all the treasures of wisdom and knowledge.

—Colossians 2:2–3

Paul's words expressed the Holy Spirit's desire that the Colossian Christians be encouraged, comforted, and fortified. This supernatural strength was transmitted through Paul's revelation of the abounding wealth provided as our heritage and legacy in Christ.

A supernatural understanding of the treasures in Christ is a deep well of assurance and spiritual conviction for a believer. The more intimate our knowledge of the mysteries and secrets of God, hidden in the Bridegroom and reserved for His bride, the deeper our faith becomes.

Twice I have had spiritual experiences in which I entered a treasury room and surveyed a portion of these awesome heavenly books. Weighty mysteries have been reserved for discovery by the end-time generation. Part of Heaven's plan is to bring a magnificent completion of the ages through an overcoming body of believers. That generation's commission will be to introduce the Lord Jesus Christ in His glory and power.

This lofty assignment is one of the many biblical reasons and admonitions for this revelatory age. To venture deep into the heart of God and discover the mind of Christ, men and women must be anointed with the spirit of revelation. From His heart, we apprehend His thoughts, feelings, and elevated purposes. This divine attribute is essential to fulfill our ultimate objectives and heavenly mandates in this strategic hour.

## Visiting a Heavenly Treasury

In November 2003 I had an exhilarating experience in a heavenly room containing treasures of incalculable value. In this visionary encounter, Wanda and I were traveling in a Western, frontier setting with a fellow minister, John Paul Jackson. He also has a commission to bring revelatory understanding of the secrets of God and has ministered as a spiritual pioneer in this arena.

As the three of us were walking along a hilly trail, the incline became steeper, and large boulders and rocks lined the path. This seemed to emulate an old Western atmosphere and symbolized uncharted territories that had been previously discovered by our historical forefathers.

After walking for a long time, we stopped for a brief moment of reflection. "When are we going to be there?" I asked. At that question, a voice descended upon us: "You *are* there." At first, we were somewhat confused; we could not see what we were pursuing. At that instant, Wanda made a strategic statement that released the anointing of the Holy Spirit, opening our spiritual eyes to the place in which we were standing.

**Opening Spiritual Eyes**
We the Church are about to apprehend the hope of our high calling. Many believers are beginning to comprehend the riches of His inheritance. We only need an impartation from Heaven to enlighten our eyes to a deep and intimate knowledge of Him.

In my vision, the three of us never moved from where we were; instead, our eyes were opened to a different realm. It was as though we had been transported from the natural world into the spiritual. Wanda's statement provided a key that opened our eyes to this awesome domain. As an intercessor, Wanda represents a spiritual key of consecrated prayer, unlocking the doors to this dimension.

When our eyes opened to this vibrant spiritual realm, we discovered that we were standing in a treasury room of

Heaven. Intuitively, we knew that we had been given access to a chamber containing objects of such incredible value that it would be impossible fully to understand their worth. It looked very similar to a great king's treasury vault.

However, the objects of unfathomable value in this room were not golden goblets or precious jewels. Rather they were scrolls, parchments, ancient books, and records. These contained the treasures of wisdom and knowledge hidden in Christ Jesus. It must have been what Paul was envisioning when he penned:

> that is, Christ Himself, in whom are hidden all the treasures of wisdom and knowledge.
> —Colossians 2:2–3

The large room was filled to capacity with incredible artifacts, including paintings and architectural blueprints, even documents containing the secrets of the universe.

**Streams of Life**
The three of us stood in what seemed to be the left side of this room. In front of us, a small stream of water flowed and separated us from the main portion of the room housing the treasures. The water coursing through this two-foot wide stream seemed to be golden in color. I am not certain if the water itself was gold or if it reflected the colors emanating from the objects in the room; nevertheless, it was stunning—we knew instinctively that it originated from the River of Life.

We were awestruck by the beauty and otherworldly wealth contained in the room. Directly in front of us was a stack of several books; each was approximately three-feet long and a foot wide. I looked intently at the cover of the one on top. I ascertained that it was made of a dark, almost black wooden material. A beautiful red design was carved into the wood. I took the top book from the stack and opened it to the first page. That single page contained volumes of knowledge involving the cellular and molecular structure of creation. There were images that demonstrated the progression and growth of a cell— information that reflected the glory of God in creation. Each portrait contained incredible detail about God's creativity.

As I observed this page, John Paul took the book from my hands, brought it close to his face and breathed deeply. When he did, I knew he had accomplished two purposes. First, it seemed to authenticate the revelation. With his breath, he inhaled the fragrance of Heaven and discerned this as a genuine revelation of Christ and His mysteries. Second, in this domain, all spiritual senses came to life.

All five spiritual senses were awakened, allowing the presence and power of God to be fully appreciated. The Holy Spirit activated the five senses so each could absorb and comprehend the revelation of divine wisdom.

It was an incredible privilege to be granted access to this treasury room. Among the riches were secrets and mysteries of Heaven greatly needed in this generation. When the Lord Jesus walked the earth, He began to reveal wisdom hidden from the foundation of the world.

All these things Jesus spoke to the multitude in parables . . . that it might be fulfilled which was spoken by the prophet, saying:

> "I will open My mouth in parables;
> I will utter things kept secret from the foundation of
> the world."
> —Matthew 13:35, NKJV

From this passage, we know that there are secrets held in

reserve from the very creation of the world. Many of those mysteries were uncovered and fulfilled by the Lord and the early apostles. Nevertheless, a reservoir remains of hidden secrets to be revealed by the mature bride just before the return of the Lord. It will be the duty and responsibility of the generations of believers alive at this time to accomplish that commission and disclose all that has been allotted for this side of eternity.

As the vision continued, I watched John Paul hold the large book firmly. Suddenly, the nail marks of the cross appeared in his hands. I knew, symbolically, that these scars illustrated the persecution and suffering he had endured. His struggle paved the way for the Lord to release a spiritual blessing to him. The Bible declares that the Lord endured the cross, despising its shame, for the joy set before Him. He was willing to suffer brutality and bloodshed in order to apprehend the prize set before Him. His suffering was rewarded and offset by the redemption of creation. With that, I came out of the experience.

**Mining the Treasures of God**
The canon of Scripture we possess contains the perfect Word of God. It is the complete revelation of Jesus Christ. Nothing can be added or removed. Nonetheless, substantial revelation, wisdom, and insight can be excavated in God to bring greater comprehension to the Scriptures and the impartation of spirit and life they convey.

The Father is pleased when His children are desperate to draw near to Him and explore His vastness. It wasn't enough for Moses to have the assurance of God's presence, he longed to understand God's ways. That cry, emanating from the depths of Moses' soul, captivated God's heart. It opened the door for a great friendship between God and Moses.

We have only just begun to mine the depths of God's Word.

Unfathomable riches of our inheritance are waiting to be secured through the Spirit. Deep wells of truth are available to this generation to make the bride ready for the Bridegroom. Intimacy with Christ embodies the very essence of our revelatory heritage. Passion and divine fellowship grow as access to spiritual treasures is given by God. As was prophetically spoken by Isaiah:

Then the eyes of those who see will not be blinded,
And the ears of those who hear will listen.
The mind of the hasty will discern the truth,
And the tongue of the stammerers will hasten to
    speak clearly.

—Isaiah 32:3–4

Eye has not seen and ear has not heard, nor has it yet entered into the heart of a person, all that God has prepared and made ready for those who love Him. Nonetheless, the bride of Christ has been promised the spirit of revelation. Revelatory gifts grant access into the depths and chambers of God's heart, revealing the boundless riches of His Kingdom.

When we are drawn to the Lord's heart, we discover His nature and character. In Him, we can explore the vastness of revelatory truth and examine things hidden beyond human scrutiny. Like the beloved apostle John, a desperate generation will lay their heads upon His chest to hear His heartbeat for a righteous and ordained day. In that place are granted revelatory encounters like those given to Daniel, John, Paul, and numerous others throughout history. His Spirit allows passage to the journals of Heaven that provide illumination and comprehension into His mysteries and spiritual wealth. This is our heritage.

The Bible announces that sound and godly wisdom is stored and hidden away, awaiting apprehension by the righteous

(Proverbs 2:7). Those who are upright and walk with the Lord in friendship will access insulated reserves containing deep things set apart for an appointed day. That day has arrived!

**Mysteries Revealed**

The prophet Daniel prophetically identified this generation and described it as the "end of time" (Daniel 12:4). He foresaw and recognized a time when spiritual knowledge would increase and great mysteries of the Kingdom would be revealed (Daniel 12). Many loyal saints are now calling upon the Lord to show great and mighty things. We desire to appreciate fully the end-time mysteries of the Kingdom.

This is the counsel of the Lord:

> "Call to Me and I will answer you, and I will tell you
> great and mighty things, which you do not know."
> —Jeremiah 33:3

We are instructed to call upon the Lord with the expectation of being heard. When we do, we will be given the ability to receive precise, clear understanding from Him. We will perceive and embody prominent and awesome mysteries of His Kingdom that are presently unknown. Then the blueprint of Heaven for this long-awaited day will be unveiled.

Access to the treasures of wisdom and knowledge resident in Christ are given in revelatory encounters—and the supernatural insight of the Spirit grants a more complete and unifying view of the Scriptures. The apostle Paul received his understanding of the gospel through a revelation of Jesus Christ. We have that same opportunity. Truth that we have only dimly seen and passages we only understand slightly will become obvious and rich through spiritual encounters with Him.

We actually know very little about the manifold deposits of truth inherent in the Scriptures. Though some may quote the Bible from cover to cover, that in itself does not constitute knowing the Living Word. Simply reciting language is not the same as comprehending truth. There are volumes of revelatory wisdom and knowledge yet to be excavated by radically hungry lovers of God.

## The End of Time
In the visitations given to Daniel, the prophet saw and heard Heaven's lofty plans for a strategic generation. He was told that his revelation was not for his day but for "the time of the end." It specifically applied to the latter-day generation. He was further instructed to close and seal the visionary disclosures he observed until the day arrived when many would be allowed to search through the heavenly book to find the knowledge it contains. Only Jesus Christ is worthy to open the seven-sealed book of redemption and disclose it to those He chooses. This book contains the complete revelation of Jesus and mysteries of the Kingdom of Heaven.

The plans, purposes, and intents of God revealed to Daniel and divinely secured in Heaven will be unveiled to this generation by the spirit of revelation. That is the prophetic promise of Scripture (Daniel 12:4).

Furthermore, the angel assured Daniel that while he would rest with his ancestors, his revelation would remain until the end-time. Many will respond to the call to pursue purity and make themselves ready for this day of visitation. Those who act wickedly will have little understanding—but the righteous will shine like a bright star. Those who possess the spirit of wisdom shall impart their divine understanding of the Kingdom realm of God (Daniel 12:9–10; 11:33–35).

It is our role to call upon the Lord from a humble and sincere heart and ask for the heavenly treasuries containing Christ's secrets and mysteries. It is His place to open the door and grant access. Only by a sovereign act of grace and power can we ascertain the mysteries we presently do not know but desperately need.

Achieving this realm in God is accomplished neither through human zeal nor soulish striving but from an honest heart desperately longing for intimacy and fellowship with Him. The enlightenment from this union will begin to uncover the riches that are our inheritance in Christ and it will reveal the sovereign strategy of Heaven for this generation.

**Books of Heaven**
The Bible depicts many heavenly books containing the records and actions of humanity. In Revelation 13:8; 17:8, and 20:12–15, we read about the Book of Life. Furthermore, we also glean from Revelation that "books" will be opened in a future day that somehow relate to the consummation of the ages and the motives, actions, and decisions of humanity. The apostle John records:

> I saw the dead, the great and the small, standing before the throne, and books were opened; and another book was opened, which is the book of life; and the dead were judged from the things which were written in the books, according to their deeds.
> —Revelation 20:12

Several books are identified in this passage, but it primarily refers to the one book containing the names of those who have embraced life in Christ—the Book of Life. The Bible specifically teaches that the Book of Life is located in Heaven. At the appropriate time, it will be displayed by the Lord at His judgment seat.

In Luke 10:17–24, we read of the return of Jesus' seventy disciples from a period of ministry. These followers marveled at the spiritual power imparted to them, noting that even evil spirits were subject to the authority of Christ in them. Jesus Himself said that He saw Satan falling like lightning because of the spiritual influence given to the disciples to tread upon serpents and scorpions.

Despite their victory, the Lord made a revealing statement:

> Nevertheless do not rejoice in this, that the spirits are subject to you, but rejoice that your names are recorded in heaven.
>
> —Luke 10:20

Many names will be found in the Book of Life from this harvest age. Soon a supernatural separation of the wheat and the tares will occur. That is the scriptural promise for the end-time. The great end-time battle between light and darkness, long foretold, will soon begin. Once the harvest is complete, the books will be closed and the next phase of God's grand plan will begin.

### Recording Heaven's Plans and Strategies

The Bible presents the Book of Remembrance and the Book of Truth, which chronicle the plans and strategies of Heaven. This generation is being offered a unique opportunity to access promises foreseen and foretold by saints and prophets of past ages. The overcoming Church is being offered an open door to apprehend greater dimensions of truth and impart them to our generation. *The Book of Remembrance*, which is mentioned in Malachi 3, contains the names of those who walk before the Lord in reverential awe and who weep over the abominations being committed in the earth.

Then those who feared the LORD spoke to one another, and the LORD gave attention and heard it, and a book of remembrance was written before Him for those who fear the LORD and who esteem His name. "They will be Mine," says the LORD of hosts, "on the day that I prepare My own possession, and I will spare them as a man spares his own son who serves him. So you will again distinguish between the righteous and the wicked, between one who serves God and one who does not serve Him." (Malachi 3:16–18)

This sacred book is endeared by the Lord. Its pages contain the names of those who faithfully join themselves to Him and who carry His heart for their generation. According to the prophetic promises in Scripture, the end-time generation is identified as the harvest of the ages. We are to carry the Lord's dominion over demons, disease, and death. Many names will be transcribed in the Book of Remembrance in this day; such people will enjoy the benefits of Heaven itself.

The apostle John and the prophet Daniel were both endowed with prophetic inspiration and recorded key mysteries that were not for their day. Instead these strategies were for our time. Their insights, sealed in the treasuries of Heaven, await the perfect timing of God. The appointed moment has now come for spiritual spies to venture into the Promised Land to taste the "grapes of Eshcol." This kingdom fruit will awaken a generation of destiny to its spiritual inheritance.

The Lord has promised that many will be allowed to search vigorously through the books containing these sealed mysteries and knowledge. Access to the esteemed secrets revealed to Daniel will increase from now until the end of the age (Daniel 12:4).

# 2

# THE BOOK
## *of* TRUTH

King David, through prophetic vision, knew that his destiny was foreseen and recorded in Heaven long before his birth. He discovered a specific and unique heavenly book, which led him to understand that his days were numbered and appointed in Heaven even before he was formed in his mother's womb. The all-knowing, all-seeing eye of God peered through the portals of time and recorded the loyal and loving actions of David. The days of King David were calculated and established for him in the books of destiny in Heaven. David put it this way:

> Your eyes have seen my unformed substance;
> And in Your book were all written
> The days that were ordained for me,
> When as yet there was not one of them.
>
> —Psalm 139:16

Many biblical scholars have difficulty with this text, but I believe it means precisely what it says. Our God is sovereign and infinite; He is not bound by the limitations of time. He can foresee every thought, decision, and action that shall ever be made. From that eternal posture, He is able to record in the journals of Heaven all the days of our individual lives. He can do this before we were even formed in our mother's womb.

Before the world itself was formed, we were in Christ. He knew His plans for us from the beginning of eternity. These plans are designed for our good (Jeremiah 29:11). God wants us to be incredibly fruitful and to prosper spiritually. He knew every person who would turn his or her attention to Him, as Moses did at the burning bush.

An eternal truth is provided in Nahum 1:7:

The LORD is good, a stronghold in the day of trouble,
And He knows those who take refuge in Him.

The Lord has known, from the beginning, who will make Him his or her refuge. All our heartaches and tears are captured and preserved in the books of Heaven (Psalm 56:8). David recognized that the persecution and hardships that he endured because of the call of God on his life did not go unnoticed by Heaven. Every tear, prayer, and proclamation in agreement with Heaven is chronicled as a precious treasure before God.

The Lord observes the activity and meditations of humanity on the earth. He is intimately involved in every facet of our existence and carefully records the wanderings of humans on the earth. As the Psalmist declared:

The LORD looks from heaven;
He sees all the sons of men;

From His dwelling place He looks out
On all the inhabitants of the earth,
He who fashions the hearts of them all,
He who understands all their works.
The king is not saved by a mighty army;
A warrior is not delivered by great strength.
A horse is a false hope for victory;
Nor does it deliver anyone by its great strength.
Behold, the eye of the LORD is on those who fear Him,
On those who hope for His lovingkindness,
To deliver their soul from death
And to keep them alive in famine.

—Psalm 33:13-19

Our destinies are securely held in the hand of God. Our primary bridal responsibility is to make ourselves ready by pursuing Him and worshipping Him in spirit and truth. From that posture, we relinquish our personal will and prophetic destiny to Him. It then becomes His responsibility and pleasure to see our destiny fulfilled and heavenly mandates accomplished. As one of our friends likes to say, "God has never faltered in one of His promises, and we will not be His first failure."

### Book of Résumés

A few years ago, while we were together at a prophetic conference in Charlotte, North Carolina, Bob Jones had a profound heavenly encounter. In it, an angel escorted him into a vast room containing a seemingly endless array of books. The journals he saw comprised the wisdom of the ages. The angel selected one of the great volumes and placed it on a wooden podium. As Bob came closer to the book, he could read the inscription on the outside—it read *Book of Résumés*.

Bob intuitively knew that the spiritual destinies of several individuals were listed in the heavenly album. In his visitation to the library, he was allowed to open the book and examine the plans of God for specific Christians. This room contained many of those heavenly aspirations and divine plans for believers, both alive today and in previous generations.

It is interesting that the book was entitled *Book of Résumés*, implying that these things had already been accomplished. A résumé is a brief account of one's professional and educational experience and qualifications, written as a summary of things achieved. Although we have yet to walk them out on earth, these things have already been completed in Heaven with the absolute cooperation of the Holy Spirit.

The *Book of Résumés* lists the spiritual accomplishments ordained for individuals. However, if disobedience or rebellion pre-empted the completion of the tasks assigned, then that individual's destiny would not be completed in that person's lifetime. In many cases, those duties and commissions were passed to someone else for their completion.

> *The spiritual tasks and responsibilities ordained for us have been recorded in Heaven's books. It is our privilege to finish faithfully the race and consummate God's allotted plans for us.*

It was Joshua, for example, who secured the inheritance for the people of Israel, even though that promise was initially offered to Moses. Moses was given the assignment to bring the people out of Egypt and lead them into the Promised Land, but the fullness of the commission was not attained in his lifetime. After the death of Moses, this call was passed on to Joshua, his spiritual son (Joshua 11:23). Similarly, Elisha carried forward the prophetic ministry originally imparted to Elijah.

Hours before His death, Jesus told the Father that He had fully accomplished the earthly work assigned to Him (John 17:9). He had glorified the Father and fully completed His appointed work. Heaven had ordained a destiny, and Jesus Christ is the perfect example of fully yielding oneself to seeing that destiny accomplished. Likewise, the apostle Paul articulated his own desire to complete the commission set before him in Heaven's blueprint:

> But I do not consider my life of any account as dear to myself, so that I may finish my course and the ministry which I received from the Lord Jesus, to testify solemnly of the gospel of the grace of God.
>
> —Acts 20:24

The spiritual tasks and responsibilities ordained for us have been recorded in Heaven's books. It is our privilege to finish faithfully the race and consummate God's allotted plans for us.

### Individual Destinies

In his visitation, Bob was allowed to read the destinies of individuals with whom he was in relationship. He observed that most had only just begun the spiritual journey assigned for them.

The first résumé he examined was his own. After comparing the things ordained for his life with those he had already accomplished, Bob realized that only a small percentage had been performed.

In this experience, he was also allowed to read the divine résumés of the apostles Paul and John. Surprisingly, Bob discovered that the spiritual assignments given to them for their generation were no greater than the ones ordained for our day.

In many cases, destinies appointed for this day had even more spiritual opportunity than the early Church. The early apostles lived at the time of birthing and sowing of Kingdom seeds. We are living in a day identified with the maturity and harvest of all seeds.

When he read the heavenly résumés of the apostles Paul and John, Bob noticed a complete page filled with supernatural exploits and accomplishments that had birthed the apostolic Church. Many items listed could be correlated with scriptural events, while others could not. It was strikingly apparent in Bob's visitation that Heaven's plans for our day are no less important. The spiritual accomplishments plotted for this generation are as significant and profound as those given to the great apostles who walked with the Lord Jesus in His earthly ministry and birthed the apostolic Church.

In this encounter, Bob was also allowed to observe the recorded destiny of a prophetic minister used mightily by the Lord through several expressions of revival. This man entered the ministry as a teenager and has served the Lord for more than fifty years. Bob marveled that those fifty-plus years only accounted for half of the ordained spiritual exploits recorded to this man's résumé. In the remaining years of his life, this humble servant of Christ will accomplish as much as he did in his first fifty. This indicates an escalation and acceleration of spiritual fruitfulness in the coming days.

*The Holy Spirit has thoroughly searched us. He knew every intimate detail of our existence before we were even born.*

The Holy Spirit has thoroughly searched us. He knew every intimate detail of our existence before we were even born. He knows when we sit down and when we arise; He understands our thoughts from an eternal perspective. The prophet David recognized this reality and acknowledged the precious value of every entry the Lord has made for us in His archives of destiny. If we were to try to count them, we would discover their number to be too great for our comprehension (Psalm 139).

## The Archives of Heaven

Roland Buck is another man who was given an opportunity to view the records of Heaven and observe the destinies of key biblical and historical figures. In his divine encounter, this dearly beloved pastor of an Assembly of God church in Boise, Idaho, was shown the heavenly accounts of Abraham, Paul, and other spiritual fathers, along with those of several key leaders in his own generation.

Pastor Buck's visitation was the first in a series of immensely meaningful experiences that included twenty-seven visitations from the angel Gabriel. In addition to the messenger angel, other ministering spirits and warring angels—including the archangel Michael—visited Buck. The profound supernatural ministry that this man released to the Church in the late 1970s marked a notable transition into a more pronounced Kingdom dimension. It was a significant sign to God's people.

Buck had served the Lord faithfully for many years as the shepherd of a small flock. Not even he could have known the supernatural experiences and prophetic ministry that would characterize the last two-and-a-half years of his life. I believe his brief, but powerfully impacting, ministry was very strategic in the scheme of Heaven and the transition into this present day.

## A Throne Room Visitation

Roland Buck's experience began on January 21, 1977. On that Saturday evening, Pastor Buck had been in his study preparing for his church's Sunday morning service. At approximately 10:30 p.m., while in prayer and meditation, he heard an audible voice say "Come with Me into the throne room, where the secrets of the universe are kept." Instantly, Pastor Buck was catapulted from his study into God's throne room.

This humble man had many incredible truths imparted to him during this throne room visitation. Greater understanding of the Scriptures was instantly grafted into his spirit. In addition, he was given the privilege of viewing the books of Heaven and the blueprint of God for this generation.

> *Even before we were fashioned in our mother's womb, these events were foreseen and inscribed in Heaven's archives.*

The books of Heaven contain the destinies of specific individuals and their endeavors, victories, and accomplishments. Even before we were fashioned in our mother's womb, these events were foreseen and inscribed in Heaven's archives. What a tremendous display of the sovereignty of God!

Pastor Buck was permitted to view partially his own heavenly résumé. In it, he was miraculously told of one-hundred and twenty future events that would transpire in his life. He later shared how the foreknowledge of these events was supernaturally imposed upon his heart and mind in complete detail and accuracy. History now records the validity of Buck's visitation as each of those circumstances unfolded, exactly according to the revelation given in his throne room visit. Only God could achieve such a feat. The odds against foretelling one-hundred and twenty future occurrences in detail—with each happening in precisely the manner described—would be incalculable. I have actually met and talked with individuals who knew him and can validate this reality firsthand.

The Lord graciously gifted Pastor Buck with insight into the destinies of people like Cyrus, Abraham, Paul, and several leaders from his own church. He was granted incredible wisdom about creation, energy, matter, and the mysteries of the universe. The Holy Spirit had something very specific in mind with the release of these revelations to Pastor Buck. He was among several forerunners, sent in the previous generation, to introduce our remarkable supernatural opportunity.

The enemy wants to heap discouragement and hopelessness on God's people through seemingly insurmountable circumstances and problems. Thankfully the Lord counters this assault: he uses hope to displace hopelessness. He gives His people vision into the thoughts and plans of His heart, sparking spiritual vitalization and expectancy in us. He highlights the wonder of divine encounters and spiritual victories destined to be shared in our day. He affords us glimpses into the depths of the love in His heart for His bride in order to awaken us from slumber and inflame us with the passions of the eternal realm.

## The Book of Truth

The prophet Daniel was highly esteemed in Heaven and privileged with a number of key visitations that directly apply to our generation. After recognizing that Israel's captivity was soon coming to an end, Daniel initiated a prayer of repentance and spiritual awakening (Daniel 9). His petition has permeated the Body of Christ for the past several years. Just as the Israelites had been in bondage for seventy years, the bride of Christ is about to be set free from bondage to experience an unprecedented spiritual awakening and restoration.

Daniel, recognizing the timing of God established through the prophet Jeremiah, positioned himself as a mediator between Heaven and earth. His life carried the burden for his people and Heaven's plan for their restoration. He touched the heart of God. As a result, the Holy Spirit used Daniel to facilitate the transition of Israel back to the place of their heritage. However, only a small remnant of people responded to the call to return and rebuild the Temple. This seemed to grieve the elderly prophet, prompting three weeks of mourning and fasting before God. The Lord responded to that sadness with a supernatural messenger who carried insight into God's plans for His people. Daniel 10 records the prominent visitation given to him:

> So he said, "Do you know why I have come to you?
> Soon I will return to fight against the prince of Persia,
> and when I go, the prince of Greece will come; but
> first I will tell you what is written in the Book of Truth.
> (No one supports me against them except Michael,
> your prince.)"
> —Daniel 10:20–21, NIV

We are not absolutely certain who Daniel encountered on that day. The wording of verses 5–9 closely resembles other depictions of the Lord Jesus in His role as the just Judge. Perhaps Daniel was given a glimpse of the Lord, along with an exchange with the archangel Gabriel. Many Bible commentators, including myself, believe it was Gabriel who delivered the messages from the Book of Truth.

This announcement required a heavenly being to impart the insight. The book from which he read was not of this world—it was from the eternal realm. The words were not of earthly origin, but they came from a heavenly library.

Our call and challenge in this day is similar to Daniel's. We must humbly present ourselves to God and receive the burden of Heaven for our generation. When we do, it will generate heavenly destinies expressed by supernatural means.

I believe that a number of people will be privileged to have similar encounters with heavenly messengers and be granted insight from the Book of Truth. These strategies, destinies, and providence must be obtained at this time.

The Book of Truth contains predetermined plans and events decreed by Heaven, which must transpire. We are privileged to be included in these plans. We enjoy eternal fruit when we offer ourselves to the Lord to assist in the accomplishment of His heavenly design. However, whether individuals cooperate and are willing to yield to the divine will is determined by our free will, combined with the grooming and preparation of the Holy Spirit for this responsibility. Ultimately, the Lord will find someone as His messenger and deliverer to bring Heaven to earth and fulfill His plan, purpose, and heavenly design.

*Ultimately, the Lord will find someone as His messenger and deliverer to bring Heaven to earth and fulfill His plan, purpose, and heavenly design.*

Jesus Christ is the same yesterday, today, and forever; this truth from Hebrews 13:8 is often quoted. However, to fully appreciate this divine promise, we must consider the preceding verse:

> Remember those who led you, who spoke the word of God to you; and considering the result of their conduct, imitate their faith. Jesus Christ is the same yesterday and today, yes and forever.
>
> —Hebrews 13:7–8

We are admonished to remember the devoted saints and leaders from prior generations who spoke the word of God and demonstrated His ways. They were the ones who paved the way for others to live in the supernatural arena of the Spirit. These privileges were not only intended for a few who lived many centuries ago; rather, these forerunners simply provided the pattern and spiritual trail for others to follow.

Hebrews 13:7–8 encourages us to consider, and observe accurately, the result of their conduct. Daniel's conduct, for example, resulted in a visitation from God and insight into the Book of Truth. When we imitate these leaders' faith, we will get the same results, because Jesus is the same yesterday, today, and forever!

One of the cornerstones of our faith is the immutability of the omnipotent God. It has been a common mistake, particularly in the Western church, to emulate the people used by God. Instead, our directive is to imitate their faith.

When we carry God's burden for our generation and for the fulfillment of heavenly mandates ordained for our time, we are poised to peer into the Book of Truth. Heavenly messengers await our responses to current needs so they can share insight from the books of Heaven. Corporate and individual destinies are launched with divine support when we live attuned to Kingdom vision and purposes. The eyes of God are roving to and fro looking for the ones whose hearts are completely His.

The Bible points to an escalation in supernatural activity in the last days, not a decrease. God's purposes for today are as significant as the transition of Israel from Babylon and the deliverance of the children of Israel from Egyptian bondage. Exponential increases in the activities of Gabriel and the hosts of Heaven—working in concert with the Holy Spirit—will occur. Great insight will be shared from the treasures hidden in Christ. The more completely we understand the divine intent, the more we can cooperate with the Spirit to release the overcoming authority of God.

## The Messenger and the Message

Gabriel brought Daniel incredible insight from a written record of truth and heavenly decrees. Only in God can these divine purposes and destinies be actualized. Scripture makes it clear that the angel came to make Heaven's plans known on earth. Access cannot be granted to those heavenly records except through supernatural impartation. A sovereign God will share future events known only to Him with those whom He highly esteems.

The messenger Gabriel is uniquely designated to announce good news and seasons of transition from Heaven to earth. He brought supernatural revelation to Daniel as Israel was about to enter a period of restoration. Likewise, he told Zacharias of the birth of his son, John the Baptist, the forerunner of Christ. Similarly, he communicated to Mary that she would conceive, by the Holy Spirit, a child who would be called Immanuel. Each of these visitations marked a profound season of transition, signifying a closing of one era and the introduction of another.

In Gabriel's encounter with Daniel, the archangel announced that he was bringing insight from the Book of Truth.

> But first I will tell you what is written in the Book of Truth. (No one supports me against them except Michael, your prince.)
>
> —Daniel 10:21, NIV

The Book of Truth is a record of God's plans, purposes, and

decrees concerning the affairs of humanity. God sees the end from the beginning and views all of time as a single moment. From His eternal perspective, the Lord records His judgments, mandates, and aspirations.

Gabriel told Daniel the future of nations, which we can now trace historically. It seems the archangel had a duty to articulate and unfold the destinies recorded in the Book of Truth.

The remainder of the book of Daniel outlined the decree of God concerning the nations of the earth—their births and downfalls and the political and spiritual implications of each—and their relationship to His covenant people. The angel imparted this information to Daniel at the time of Israel's passage from captivity into a promised recovery. Gabriel delivered discernment and comprehension about the Lord's plan. The Bible declares that the vision and strategy pertained to "the days yet future" (Daniel 10:14)—our day.

**From Two Witnesses**
In December 2000 I was part of a prophetic conference team that also included Bob Jones, Bobby Connor, Todd Bentley, and John Paul Jackson. In an effort to stop God's purposes for this conference, the enemy had dwarfed the entire area of southern Oregon in a thick fog bank that remained for two full days. Meteorologists confirmed it was one of the oddest displays of intense fog they had ever witnessed.

As a result, our flight from Seattle into Medford was turned away during our approach. My wife, Wanda, and I ended up spending an extra night in Portland, hoping to complete the trip the next day. Unfortunately, many flights had been canceled in that area. When we returned to the airport the next morning, chaos and confusion abounded. Many travelers openly expressed their anger and frustration. The gate area was congested and noisy. It was definitely an unfavorable spiritual atmosphere.

Somehow amidst the clamor and frustration, the Lord spoke to me in a profound way. Clearly and concisely He said, "I am beginning to reveal things from the Book of Truth." With that word, I was also given Daniel 10:21. I wrote the expression and biblical reference on a piece of paper and placed it in the back of my Bible.

After another attempted flight we were still unable to land in Medford. We finally rented a vehicle and drove to the conference. The next morning, focused fully on the conference, I had completely set aside the message from the day before. While Todd Bentley preached that morning, Bobby Connor took my Bible and began to thumb through the pages. I assumed he wanted to read a certain Scripture from a different translation.

> *Somehow amidst the clamor and frustration, the Lord spoke to me in a profound way. Clearly and concisely He said, "I am beginning to reveal things from the Book of Truth."*

Bobby plopped my Bible back in my lap and pointed his finger at the Scripture he had located. It was Daniel 10:21. He said, "The Lord is about to speak to us from the Book of Truth." That was a WOW moment. Not even my wife, Wanda, knew about the directive the Holy Spirit had given me. I withdrew the piece of paper from my notes confirming the same message from the day before.

It was an incredible validation from the Lord regarding His promise to speak to us about the mysteries and destinies contained in this strategic book. From the mouths of two witnesses, the word was established.

Destiny is being revealed as we broach a "fullness of time" juncture in church history and in the plan of God. These are pivotal days as we progressively shift into a fresh mode of Heaven and the Kingdom realm.

CHAPTER

3

# SEASONS *of* TRANSITION

s with Daniel's Israel, we have been in a season of transition. The Church is moving into a new day of intense revelation from the Kingdom of Heaven. The Lord's dominion, achieved through His great victory, will soon unfold before our very eyes. It will be the bride's revival, where Jesus will fully live in a body of people and do, through them, the same works that He did while on the earth in human form. As with Israel at the time of their Babylonian release, we too have been privileged with a visitation by the archangel Gabriel to help in this transitional season.

Roland Buck was highly esteemed by God and granted an incredible journey to God's throne room. There he received amazing insight in God's archives. He also received twenty-seven visitations from the angel Gabriel. Clearly something of vital spiritual importance transpired during that two-year season.

It is not my intention to overemphasize the ministry and function of angels. They function merely as messengers of God, but the message they carry is profound.

The Bible is filled with human encounters with heavenly beings, which usually happened at crucial times of deliverance, judgment, and restoration. God's relationship with humanity has not changed. What is the Lord saying to us? What was the strategy of Heaven in releasing this series of visitations, beginning in 1977?

To answer these questions thoroughly, we must look at previous generations and carefully examine the expression of the Holy Spirit to leaders in those days. That was Daniel's approach, as recorded in Daniel 9. To understand what God was saying to his generation, Daniel contemplated the prophetic directives given years before through Jeremiah.

To be entrusted with more wisdom, we must faithfully steward and administer the prophetic deposits of God. When Joshua led the Israelites into the Promised Land, he wisely and dutifully served Moses and the revelation of Heaven according to Moses. Stewardship of already-revealed spiritual truth allowed God to bless Joshua with the same spirit that was on Moses, even though that spirit exhibited different attributes of God's divine nature. Joshua was then able to complete the plan and promise of God for his day.

In much the same way, our decision to appreciate and apply God's benefits from previous days may result in a commission like Joshua's. We too could see the awesome Warrior God, the Captain of the Lord's Hosts, displayed before us.

Incredible prophetic missions affirmed through signs and wonders were fulfilled in the previous generation through the ministries of several devoted saints. Their prophetic messages are signposts validated by God that will build a platform for the latter day army to arise in power and authority.

## Signs from Heaven

Many amazing signs, recorded in both Christian and secular media, occurred during the twentieth century. Several of those phenomena were witnessed by thousands, many of whom are still alive today. I have had the privilege of speaking with a number of people who saw tremendous displays of God's power. We would be wise to examine accounts of those wonders carefully in order to extract their spiritual application for our day. While reviewing these wonders, it is important not to elevate any human instrument but rather to seek to understand God's message by it and its significance.

## A Forerunner Ministry

During the early 1930s a greatly gifted prophet William Branham was shown incredible future events that have already become a matter of historical record.

Following a series of evangelistic meetings, Branham held a baptismal service on June 11, 1933, for new converts. Some four thousand people lined the banks of the Ohio River to observe and celebrate the service. While baptizing the seventeenth person, a whirling amber light descended from Heaven and rested directly above Branham. Virtually all the witnesses present could see this supernatural sign. Many eyewitnesses ran in fear, while others fell to their knees and worshipped because they recognized this was God doing something truly extraordinary.

God gave William Branham a forerunner message for his life and ministry. I believe he was a token or prototype of an entire body of people who will emerge as Jesus' bridal company. By his own acknowledgment, Branham was a harbinger of something new and fresh the Lord planned for the last days. This supernatural dimension will be commonplace in end-time life and ministry.

Many secular North American newspapers carried the story of the light, as reported by the Associated Press. One newspaper headline read, MYSTERIOUS LIGHT APPEARS OVER BAPTIST PREACHER.

This public display of God's awesome power framed a heavenly intention. No design of Heaven is ever administered futilely. Every word and demonstration that proceeds from the mouth and hand of God will return fruitfully. A Kingdom message for today's Church was sent to that prior generation—and we are responsible for its consummation. The Living Word desires to rest in His bride. Jesus wants to become flesh once more and demonstrate His Kingdom power and redemptive virtue.

### Early Supernatural Models

If that episode on the Ohio River was just an isolated incident then we could be thrilled by such a display of God's power and move on. However, that was only one of many expressions of God in the life of this forerunner.

During his early ministry, Branham had several supernatural experiences for which he had no frame of reference or ability to understand. Neither he nor those with whom he was in ministry relationship comprehended the revelatory realm of God. Only the Bible provided any source of enlightenment; very few people had personally experienced this supernatural dimension of God. Unfortunately, most Christians at the time believed those kinds of expressions had happened in the Bible but did not any longer. Words like *trance* and *vision* rarely existed in the spiritual vocabulary of that day.

The years after World War I were difficult. Few people had access to libraries or Christian material. Branham, raised in extreme poverty in the hills of Kentucky, certainly had no way of researching how God's supernatural power had manifested throughout Church history. Nonetheless, the Spirit showed him things that would occur in the future. He shared those encounters openly with those around him. To everyone's amazement, the events came to pass in precisely the manner he predicted. Tremendous healings frequently accompanied his revelatory experiences.

It wasn't until an angelic visitation on May 7, 1946, though, that Branham came to understand more fully the purpose and validity of the supernatural dimension into which he had been thrust. This minister of God was desperate to understand the spiritual realms he was witnessing or he would die trying. He set his intent on discovering whether his visions and trances were from God or from the enemy. He loved the Lord too much to allow deception to rule him.

Branham withdrew to a secluded wooded area in rural Indiana. There was no food, electricity, or other provision. All he did was lay before God in humility and sincerity. Wonderfully, the Lord answered the cry of His servant.

An angel was sent in a tangible form to Branham and told him about his life and calling. This heavenly messenger came to impart spiritual understanding and a divine commission.

According to Branham's personal testimony, which he often shared publicly during the late '40s and throughout the '50s, something supernatural occurred late one night after many hours of prayer. A heavenly light appeared; it looked like an amber or emerald star of fire, illuminating the room around him. It was the same manifestation that had appeared over the Ohio River thirteen years earlier. At that moment

Branham heard footsteps walking toward him and saw some-one standing in the light.

An angelic messenger greeted him as in the Bible: "Fear not, for I am sent from the presence of Almighty God." The angel, according to Branham, was six feet tall and weighed approximately two hundred pounds. He had an olive complexion, with dark hair that touched his shoulders, and he wore a white robe that reached to his feet. As soon as Branham heard the greeting, he recognized the angel's voice as the one he had heard throughout his youth and early ministry.

*An appointed juncture in Church history had arrived. The Lord was looking for a messenger to fulfill a divine mandate and to introduce the supernatural dimension of Heaven to a new generation.*

An appointed juncture in Church history had arrived. The Lord was looking for a messenger to fulfill a divine mandate and to introduce the supernatural dimension of Heaven to a new generation. Clearly the humility and devotion of Branham captured Heaven's attention and opened the door for this man to be used in significant ways. A plan, initiated before the foundation of the world, was set in motion for him. The time had arrived for destiny to be fulfilled.

The angel informed Branham that he was called to take a message of divine healing around the world. The angel promised him that if he could get people to believe, nothing would hinder the fulfillment of his prayers—not even cancer. Branham introduced his generation, and ours, to the revelatory realm of Heaven. These signs and wonders acted as a platform to birth faith in the supernatural power of God.

Notable supernatural impartation was released during this

visitation. The angel told him that just like Moses, he would be given two gifts as signs of this impartation. Whenever he took a person's right hand with his left, he would by divine revelation perceive the person's physical condition. This was the first spiritual gift: it allowed the minister to detect through revelatory insight the specific illnesses, demonic oppressions, and deadly diseases afflicting the people.

Whenever Branham prophesied a precise illness or condition, his listeners' faith in God was elevated, allowing incredible healing and miracles. His first public healing meeting after his commissioning took place on June 14, 1945, in St. Louis, Missouri. Immediately creative miracles and phenomenal demonstrations of healing were generated on such a massive scale that theologians termed it an unprecedented event in Church history. As Gordon Lindsay once said, "there were no hard cases." No matter how severe the malady, the Lord was present to heal.

*This was the first spiritual gift: it allowed the minister to detect through revelatory insight the specific illnesses, demonic oppressions, and deadly diseases afflicting the people.*

The angel promised Branham that God would give him a second gift if he used the first with humility. The next gift gave him discernment of thoughts and secrets of the heart and would take people to an even deeper level of faith.

As Jesus' encounter with the Samaritan woman at the well had, the unfolding of personal history and intimate secrets ignited faith. People rose above shame and unbelief and engaged the revelatory realm of Heaven. Their response is a prophetic model for our generation.

The Bible declares that the living Word is alive, active, and a discerner of the thoughts and desires of the heart (Hebrews 4:12). The gift of discernment offers a far greater dimension in God than the expression of a simple "word of knowledge." It is a reflection that the Lord has removed the veil dividing soul and spirit, and all things are open and exposed to Him.

When operating in the gift of revelatory discernment, Branham would stand before the people and communicate, by supernatural insight, their name, illness, history, address, private prayers and desires, and many other secrets known only to the Lord. Those present in those meetings testify that this dimension of God generated a tangible expectation of faith. People believed that anything was possible in such an atmosphere of heavenly anointing.

The messenger from Heaven shared many things with Branham during their lengthy conversation. Branham's ministry introduced a different dimension in God, not seen or demonstrated on such a scale at any time throughout Church history. Its foundation was a union with Christ, with the Lord living in the midst of His people and doing, through them, the same works that He did while on earth.

## Igniting Revival

Following his angelic encounter, Brother Branham emerged with a deep anointing of revelation and power that directly or indirectly touched millions of people and launched a worldwide revival. Countless thousands were miraculously healed of the most hideous infirmities and deadly diseases during the ministry of this man and others who followed.

Naturally God puts His great treasures in earthen vessels. Like all human beings—with the exception of Jesus Christ—Brother Branham made mistakes and missteps along the way. Even so, his revelatory encounters were marked with uncanny accuracy. It is the revelation of Heaven that is of paramount importance. But just as important is the proper stewardship of the treasures of insight and wisdom with application today; we must carefully unfold God's blueprint.

A divine presence distinguished Branham's life and ministry. The living Word discerned, and communicated through Branham, the thoughts of the heart with profound precision. He was given glimpses into the plan and destiny of Heaven for individuals and corporate bodies. His forerunner ministry foresaw the impact of a body of believers who will emerge in our day and embody the living Word. The signs and wonders that follow will release a bridal revival that will be identified according to John 14:12—a "greater works" generation.

## Extracting Understanding

It is always wonderful to recount stories of God's goodness to people. However, there is much more for us to understand about God's dealings with Branham's generation. A platform had been established for heavenly truth, and we must comprehend the significance of this type of ministry for our generation. These events were much more than revival; they were the beginning of end-time ministry; they pointed to a generation of destiny prophesied in Scripture. As with Moses, these signs were given so that the people would believe.

The time has come to revisit the awesome visions given to this godly man, along with the other pieces of the divine puzzle entrusted to other Christians. Like Daniel studying the prophecies of Jeremiah, we should meditate upon these supernatural encounters to extract their application to both Branham's time and our own. We can learn from past mistakes and extract the seeds of God, replanting them in the soil of our honest and sincere hearts.

As in the days of Moses and the Lord Jesus, the enemy recognizes times and seasons that mark the appearance of spiritual deliverers. Rampant abortion, murder, and suicide should be a clear indication of the efforts used by the enemy to stop the emergence of mighty spiritual warriors. He wants to snuff out those endowed with the virtue of Heaven to carry out the plan of God.

A day of destiny is upon us. The "victorious ones" mentioned in the prophecies of Joel are being prepared to emerge as an army, the bridal company joined to the Bridegroom.

**Ending an Age**
With that brief history in mind, we should revisit a trance given to William Branham in June 1933.

On that day he was taken in the Spirit and told of Mussolini's impending invasion of Ethiopia and eventual death in 1945. Branham was shown that an Austrian named Hitler would rise as dictator of Germany and lead the world into another war. He was also shown that America would be drawn into a Second World War under Roosevelt's leadership and likewise saw a specific location where many Americans would die in battle—a prophetic picture of the place known as the Siegfried line.

Furthermore, the vision emphasized that there were three "isms"—fascism, Nazism, and communism—to watch for. The first two would come to naught, he was told, but communism would continue to flourish after the war. He was specifically informed that Russia would play a prominent role as a world power in the future.

Along with the political events, other insights were given concerning science, the moral decline of the nations, and the spiritual compromise and confrontations of the Western Church. All these spiritual forecasts were shared publicly years before they actually occurred.

In one insight, Branham was given the year 1977 as a pivotal time. Although he acknowledged that he didn't understand the full implications of that year, Branham predicted that something major would occur in 1977 to mark the end of the Laodicean church age. He was careful to note that the prediction was not a "thus saith the Lord" like the other world events revealed in the trance, but rather a calculation based on the insight from the revelations.

As the years passed, this personal prediction prompted a lot of misunderstanding. Many people believed that he was foretelling the rapture of the Church or the return of Christ. However, that was not what he had stated and, furthermore, the Bible plainly declares that we will not know the day nor the hour of those events.

Something spiritually profound did occur in 1977, though. God had a grand design that was meticulously falling into place for a future generation through the numerous supernatural wonders He was performing. Great spiritual investments were being made to position us for an inevitable day of destiny. The transition into our day had begun.

**In the Year 1977**
In 1977 Roland Buck visited Heaven's throne room, initiating a string of visitations from the angel Gabriel. On twenty-seven separate occasions, this archangel, often accompanied by other ministering spirits and warring angels, visited with Buck.

In October 2002 Wanda and I had the privilege of spending a morning with Roland Buck's widow and daughter in Boise, Idaho. They shared with us some of the highlights of Buck's encounters with the messengers from Heaven, and unquestionably something of notable prophetic consequence occurred during those few years. An appointed time, set by the

Father Himself, had arrived, for in Buck our Lord found the qualities He desired.

If the angel Gabriel is sent as a messenger, it behooves us to discover the heart and strategy of the Father in that endeavor. The Bible records that universal transitions and transformations occur following visitations with this particular angel. While we only desire Jesus Christ and the life He gives us, history clearly indicates that significant world events occur when we encounter high-ranking spiritual beings like Gabriel and Michael. That pattern continues today.

**Heavenly Directives**

The angelic messenger told Buck many of God's plans in preparation for the latter-day confrontation with darkness. Gabriel highlighted emphatically the power of redemption purchased through the blood of Jesus Christ. He stressed that very few Christians fully comprehend or appropriate the power imparted to them through heavenly grace. Many walk well below their allotted provision because of deceptive and seductive spirits that steal their heritage in Christ.

> *The Lord Jesus is looking to sanctify wholly the spirit, soul, and body of a company of believers and take up residence in them to do greater works.*

Buck was also informed of Heaven's concentrated efforts to bring workers into the Kingdom in preparation for a great harvest. He was shown how angels are assigned to labor together with the saints; when believers pray earnestly for loved ones' salvation, angels—working in cooperation with the Holy Spirit—are empowered to awaken the lost.

Throughout the visitations, Gabriel emphasized the importance of communion with Christ and intimate fellowship with God. The Lord Jesus is looking to sanctify wholly the spirit, soul, and body of a company of believers and take up residence in them to do greater works. Yet Heaven's endowment for these greater works will only be unleashed by radical intimacy and friendship with God. Waiting on the Lord will be the key to launching many into the mystical realms of Heaven.

Gabriel also highlighted the prophetic implications of the feasts of Israel. The careful and meticulous plan of Heaven is being carried out. The Lord has provided the blueprint through His Word, and now revelation and insight are being apportioned and authority delegated to actualize that Word. Clearly the visitations of the archangel Gabriel were addressing the maturing of the times and the emergence of the saints.

Buck's experiences marked a transition from what has been known as the Church ages into a more complete revelation of the Kingdom realm. Most importantly, it marked the passage into a day when the fullness of the overcoming King will be introduced. We are entering the days in which we will taste the good word of God and the powers of the age to come. Fresh releases of power and authority are being entrusted to an overcoming body of believers. We must claim this revelation of Heaven and walk in the destiny ordained for this season.

### The Cause of Heaven

God does not haphazardly send heavenly beings; He always has an awesome spiritual purpose to accomplish. A sign of the times was furnished and a series of mandates, reports, and instructions were given. When the Lord chose Roland Buck to achieve a specific task that was absolutely vital to Heaven's plans, Buck's divine encounters marked a season of transition, advancement, and refinement.

The Church's call during this present season has been to facilitate the emergence of and mobilize this new generation so its members may live in liberty, freedom, and spiritual rest. Such is the heritage promised to those betrothed to the Lord Jesus and who taste the powers of His Kingdom age.

For the most part, the corporate body has missed the incredible implications of these visitations pointing to this significant call. When the Lord tangibly sends an archangel on a single mission to meet a leader or leaders face-to-face, something outstanding, with powerful spiritual implications, is on the horizon. That is the clear pattern of Scripture. How much more so if such encounters are given twenty-seven times in less than three years! As my friend Bobby Connor likes to say, "Something's up!"

The Lord Jesus is restoring His Temple and building His Church with a Kingdom emphasis. This means that while previous emphasis has been placed on church buildings, programs, denominations, and institutions, the focus now needs to be placed on the revelation of Jesus Christ as the overcoming King. The Lord is coming *to* His people before He comes *for* them.

**Kingdom Ministry**

In times past there have been misappropriations and excesses concerning biblical truth and the ministry of the Kingdom on earth. To align us with God's Word, and to bring us back into proper order and balance, a number of vital scriptural promises must be restored. These include but are not limited to:

1. Kingdom theology
2. Discipleship
3. Manifested sons of God
4. The faith message

A true manifestation and revelation of the Kingdom realm, formed within its proper biblical boundaries, is coming. It is the revelation of Jesus Christ in and through a body of people. The Lord repeatedly proclaimed that He came to reveal the Kingdom of Heaven. Likewise, that is our mandate. But the Kingdom of Heaven is not a democracy—it is a theocracy. The Lord is King and Head, and we are joined with Him to function under His protection, authority, and leadership.

The Kingdom of God is not exclusively a heavenly domain, although Heaven is a part of the Kingdom; the Kingdom realm is much more than just a heavenly residence. God's Kingdom demonstrates the virtue of our overcoming King and His dominion in and through His people. People can go to Heaven yet never actually experience the revelation of the Kingdom in their lifetime. Fortunately Scripture promises that a victorious body of believers will taste the good Word of God and the Kingdom powers of the age to come (Hebrews 6:5).

*The penitent thief on the cross was promised entrance to Heaven even though he had neither experienced nor evidenced the Kingdom of Heaven on earth.*

The penitent thief on the cross was promised entrance to Heaven even though he had neither experienced nor evidenced the Kingdom of Heaven on earth. The Israelites spent forty years in the wilderness witnessing some of the most amazing demonstrations of heavenly power ever presented, yet still they did not come to know God. They observed the power of the Kingdom but did not enter in to an experiential oneness with Heaven to fulfill the mandates set before them. They saw the Lord's power but did not discover His ways. The Kingdom is not just about carrying the power and virtue of Heaven—it is about living in Christ's ways and rest and exemplifying His character.

Philip the evangelist experienced this dimension of God when he was instantly transported thirty miles from his encounter with an Ethiopian eunuch to Azotus. Likewise, Peter was filled with the Holy Spirit and saturated with Kingdom power. The glory emanating from him healed the sick as he walked the streets of Jerusalem.

Paul explored this realm and experienced bountiful visions and revelations of the Lord. These—and more—are the revelations of the Kingdom to be imparted in our day. The promise spoken of by Paul and foreseen by prophets is the Kingdom reality that manifests when the Lord rests in people.

# CHAPTER 4

# QUALIFYING *for* DIVINE DESTINY

I n Heaven volumes of books record the activities of humanity on the earth. Persecutions, oppressions, and injustices committed against the righteous have been carefully observed, tabulated, and sealed in the treasuries of Heaven. According to Moses:

> Their wine is the venom of serpents,
> And the deadly poison of cobras.
> Is it not laid up in store with Me,
> Sealed up in My treasuries?
>
> —Deuteronomy 32:33–34

Meticulous notations are also made of every noble decision made in accordance with God's nature and in agreement with Heaven. When humans cooperate with God and take steps of great spiritual significance, those actions are transcribed in Heaven's archives. The Book of Remembrance is a sacred and highly esteemed record of individuals who carried the burden of God in their day.

Every believer in Christ should desire to increase the books of Heaven by living a Kingdom lifestyle. Manifesting the Kingdom realm on earth is a fundamental component of the purpose of our salvation. That is exactly what Jesus came to introduce. He taught the people of Judea and declared the message of the Kingdom. He healed all manner of sickness and disease (Matthew 4:23). We have the same commission.

*We should all have a holy desire to see our names transcribed in the heavenly journals. When the books are opened, may deeds of faithfulness and loyalty performed in our generation be what is recounted.*

We should all have a holy desire to see our names transcribed in the heavenly journals. When the books are opened, may deeds of faithfulness and loyalty performed in our generation be what is recounted. When we cooperate with the Lord, treasures of gold, silver, and precious stones are generated. These spiritual jewels endure the consuming fire of God. Meanwhile, agendas and ambitions of the soul are incinerated like dry grass.

For the righteous, only fruitfulness will remain. All our mistakes and miscalculations will be erased and washed away through the blood of Jesus. That is the grace afforded through Jesus' redemption.

A righteous yearning is being imparted to the bride to do things so pleasing to Jesus that they are registered in Heaven. Many are desperate to qualify and overcome; they long to share in the blessings of victory and join the ranks of God's end-time army. The father of lies has tried to crush this plan with overwhelming waves of insufficiency and disqualification. We cannot come to agree with those demonic mind-sets.

Look at the apostle Peter and all of the mistakes he made. Nevertheless, he also did something right: He caught the Lord's attention through some virtue resident in his heart, something that qualified him for the Lord's grace. His faith in God's mercy exceeded his belief in the lies of the devil.

Consider the apostle Paul. What was it the Lord saw in him? Something in Paul agreed so fervently with the purposes of Heaven that it compensated for all the atrocities and persecutions he committed as a religious zealot. The Lord was able to take radical religious zeal and transmute it to godly passion. Saul the Pharisee became Paul the apostle of Jesus Christ. The impact and spiritual ramifications of that transition continue to resound in heavenly places. Heaven is looking for people through whom the Lord will have the liberty and freedom to fulfill God's promises for this generation. The Lord shall once again make His name famous in the earth.

For the past several years, we have been in a season of preparation. Since 1996 a measure of completion has been exhibited in the development of a body of people who have yielded themselves to the Lord. When Adam was first created, God was fully enthroned within his soul. God maintained complete dominion over every area of Adam's life. However, with the fall in the Garden of Eden, other idols began to dethrone the Lord. From that time until now God has been longing for the return of His perfect dominion inside humans. This is the whole purpose of redemption—to have the Lord enthroned in the human soul to exercise complete supremacy in every arena of life.

The Lord wants every ounce of our existence fully yielded to Him. This submission is accomplished when our spirit, soul, and body experience the complete work of redemption. Then, we are able to gaze directly into the face of God without shame or reservation. We are once again released to walk with Him in the cool of the day as Adam did (Genesis 3:8). God is so hungry for this intimacy that He seeded a prophecy to Zechariah about it. He is the Light in our evening time:

> For it will be a unique day which is known to the LORD, neither day nor night, but it will come about that at evening time there will be light.
> —Zechariah 14:7

Today is the "evening time" of human history. As with the path of the sun, civilization has moved perpetually from the east to the west. We have now gone as far west as possible; to go any further returns us to the east. The Gospel has likewise progressed from the east to the west. Every revival throughout history has migrated further to the west and completely spanned the breadth of our world. Israel has begun to be reinstituted as the promised homeland. It's evening time—the sun is setting. But a fresh day is dawning: we know by the Scriptures that there is going to be light in the evening time.

## Dawning of Kingdom Reality

The Body of Christ is on the threshold of a new day. However, in a broader sense, it is also the evening time of human history. All the end-time promises that have been spoken through the prophets and patriarchs are about to be fulfilled on the earth! Demonstrations of the Spirit will flow through people who have been set apart and prepared for this day. Measures of divine authority and redemptive virtue will rest on men and women.

Specially prepared spiritual endowments have been hidden and set aside for this hour. They are so rich and deep that the human heart hasn't even dreamed of them. These gifts have been securely held deep in the heart of God. If these Kingdom mysteries had not been hidden, they would have been perverted by the human mind throughout the generations. That is why Daniel's revelation was sealed all those centuries ago.

Heaven wisely safeguarded the apocalyptic plans that John was permitted to see. During his revelation John observed great mysteries unfolding through the seven seals and heard awesome insight in the seven thunders that spoke. However, John was forbidden to write the meaning of those penetrating revelatory images. They were hidden for a day to be determined by God Himself—our day!

If Daniel or John had written everything they had seen and heard, the precious and mysterious plan of God would have been misunderstood in a storm of confusion. Instead God planned to give a spirit of revelation to a specific generation. This discernment would allow those believers to understand these mysteries and apply them on earth.

When that day arrives, it is going to be like fresh manna falling from Heaven; God will further illuminate His Scriptures and reveal His plan to us. The power of God's heavenly commissions, as well as the speed with which the end times will unfold, will prevent the enemy from perverting, distorting, or counterfeiting these revelations. The enemy will be unable to distort their proper biblical parameters. Those devoted saints possessing spiritual eyes to see and ears to hear will be marvelously used by the Spirit. It will be a new, fresh, and powerful time.

No one will be able to say "I knew these things already!" This move of God is being forged now by the spirit of prophecy. We are now living in the day of the fulfillment of what has been foretold. New understanding will emerge from the Spirit of Truth. The strategic keys to the Kingdom are now being used to open the gates of the wonderful plan of Heaven. A more complete view of the redemptive promises outlined in Scripture is being given. The prophet Isaiah saw this day and prophesied of this anointing when he said:

You have heard; look at all this.
And you, will you not declare it?
I proclaim to you new things from this time,
Even hidden things which you have not known.
They are created now and not long ago;
And before today you have not heard them,
So that you will not say, "Behold, I knew them."
—Isaiah 48:6–7

The Church has experienced diverse expressions of revival, renewal, and spiritual outpourings in recent years. Differing standards have been implemented to gauge the seeming success of meetings. In some instances our success has been measured by how many people received personal prophetic words. Oftentimes renewal was exemplified by an altar covered with bodies. While each scenario may be a fruitful expression of God and an important part of our spiritual heritage, something different is on the horizon.

**True Spiritual Measurement**
The great interest and awakening in prophetic ministry over recent years has occurred for several reasons. Clearly personal

prophetic ministry has its place and will continue to be a vital part of true Christianity. However, that is only one of the crucial elements of the revelatory anointing being deposited in God's people. The understanding of end-time mysteries and the prophetic fulfillment of heavenly mandates will likewise be secured through this heritage.

Our measurement for a successful conference or series of meetings will change in the coming days. Previously a successful meeting was determined by the number of people slain in the spirit or experiencing some tangible manifestation of God's power. These aspects will continue to be a part of what the Lord does. But soon the greatest determination of a successful meeting will be the lasting fruit evident and the amount of displacement of darkness into light in heavenly places.

When hope displaces hopelessness and people experience this tangible change, the spiritual atmosphere has been altered by Heaven. When one is endowed with revelatory anointing, access, and vision to this realm is given—this authority allows incredible spiritual accuracy. Because we understand more of God's plan, we are better equipped to identify the enemy's strongholds and fortresses and wage war accordingly. When a realm of darkness is displaced, it is then replaced with a virtue of Christ and the Kingdom of Heaven. Territories of fears are vanquished by deposits of faith. Hopelessness is overwhelmed by hope; darkness is overcome by light.

A shift is presently taking place in the realm of the Spirit, and an unseen evaluation can now be readily discerned. This determination is made by how much "ground" has been taken in the Spirit. The evidence of true spiritual impartation has changed. We must now ask:

How many lives have been altered by what occurred in
that service?

Has anyone's prayer life been infused with life and
vibrancy?

Is there anyone who no longer experiences the same
outbursts of anger as they did before?

How many spiritual prisoners have emerged from the
dungeons of darkness to embrace the Light of
Christ and His salvation?

Has crime in the surrounding areas been reduced as a
result of God's touch on individual people?

Have the number of abortions in the surrounding
areas been reduced as a result of God's touch on
individual people?

Entire cities experience and reap the benefits of the spiritual transformations that follow these displacements through the anointing and authority of the King. A measure of darkness is scaled away, and light is birthed. That is the formula for sweeping revival and the harvest of souls.

Psalm 103:20–21 highlights this spiritual war. In that domain, angelic hosts of Light, energized by the prayer and righteousness of the saints, war with spirits of darkness determined to undermine the purposes of God. When darkness is overcome, there is a tangible shift in heavenly places that affects the natural realm.

Bless the LORD, you His angels,
Mighty in strength, who perform His word,
Obeying the voice of His word!
Bless the LORD, all you His hosts,
You who serve Him, doing His will.

Bless the LORD, all you works of His,
In all places of His dominion;
Bless the LORD, O my soul!

—Psalm 103:20–22

The areas where the enemy has previously prevailed and formed a dominion over a region, church, or family are now being displaced. In their stead, standards of righteousness are being lifted up. Areas previously known for their darkness and corruption will now become beacons of light, full of hope, faith, and purity.

True change takes place in the spirit, and the fruit of that shift blossoms in the natural. That shift is the revelation of the Kingdom of Heaven and the dominion of Christ. An early Church apostle could visit a city like Ephesus and turn it upside down with the revelation of the Kingdom, even though it had been steeped in paganism for many centuries.

Ephesus was a prosperous, influential, and wealthy region known for its worship of the false goddess Diana. In fact, a great temple built in her honor was one of the Seven Wonders of the World. But that city didn't stand a chance against the apostle Paul and the revelation of Jesus Christ he carried. The Bible records that the ministry of Paul radically altered the Ephesian mode of worship through the preaching of the gospel and the demonstration of Kingdom power. For two years he faithfully served the Lord in this way until "all who lived in Asia heard the word of the Lord, both Jews and Greeks" (Acts 19:10).

## The Humble and Contrite

People who have been given true spiritual authority in the heavenly realms are, like Paul, righteous and just. They possess humble and contrite hearts; the Lord is building a home in them where He can rest (Isaiah 66:1–2). The Lord will use those whose humble and contrite spirit trembles at His word.

Scientists have recently conducted tests and measurements in outer space and have reported fascinating results. They have used highly sensitive recording equipment to measure the "sound" of empty space. To their amazement, they have discovered that the vastness of space actually has a discernible sound. When amplified, a distinguishable rumble can be detected in the vacuum. I believe that space is still trembling from the Word of God in the very beginning of Creation. God's words "Let there be . . ." can still be heard.

*I believe that space is still trembling from the Word of God in the very beginning of Creation. God's words "Let there be . . ." can still be heard.*

Science has also developed instruments that can acutely analyze stationary rocks. Interestingly they have discovered that the rocks are trembling and vibrating. I believe creation continues to tremble at the Word of the One who spoke it into existence. Everything in nature is obedient to God's word—except humankind. However, in the last days, He will have a company of people who tremble at His word—of humble and contrite souls covered by a canopy of spiritual understanding.

"Is there not a cause?" was young David's proclamation when he heard the name of God being ridiculed by an enemy. A radical generation is emerging with hearts after God; like David, they ask the same question.

Many in our generation are crying out: "Show me a cause worth dying for, and I will live for it the rest of my life." Indeed there is a cause worth dying for! If it's worth dying for, we might as well live for it! This cause is worth giving up everything in order to accomplish it. It is worth dying to the delights of this world. It is worth living fully embracing its cause, because its fruit will be eternal. Its everlasting consequences, experienced in this day and in the age to come, will be the determining factors in many lives.

We are now living in a time foreseen by the biblical prophets; a day identified with a touch and plan of God so profound, they simply called it "the promise." According to Hebrews:

All these, having gained approval through their faith, did not receive what was promised, because God had provided something better for us, so that apart from us they would not be made perfect.

—Hebrews 11:39–40

The Bible plainly illustrates that a certain generation will come to know the reality and fullness of "the promise." The "promise" is the Lord Himself assuming residence in His people. He will dwell fully in their spirit, soul, and body, doing through them everything He has foretold. They will be a "greater works" generation.

## A Hungry Generation

A Kingdom dimension is being imparted to the Church of our day. God's cause is worth living for and giving up everything to accomplish. A company of people is being raised up—sons and daughters of God who hunger for what is real and true. A cheap imitation will not do. For them there must be a demonstration of the Spirit and power that transcends words and becomes a living reality.

Experiential authenticity is what identifies this hungry generation—they long to be a tangible representation of God on

the earth. That is the clarion call of this day and the only standard by which true spirituality can be measured.

To fulfill this appointment with destiny, the Lord is looking
for hearts filled with sincerity and grounded in truth. As we cul-
tivate these attributes through our divine exchange with the Holy
Spirit, we will be strengthened and promoted in God's army.

As the Lord Jesus expressed in His earthly ministry, the
Kingdom of Heaven is a spiritual domain. God wants us to
rule and reign with Him in heavenly places, both in this present age and in the age to come. The Bible depicts two distinct
groups emerging from the Gentile nations: One is sitting with
Him on His throne as priests and kings who reign together
with Him; the other stands before Him to serve Him day and
night. The first has a Kingdom position of authority imparted
to them as those who have overcome.

Just as Eve was formed from the rib of Adam, so also will
the bride of Christ be bone of His bone and flesh of His flesh.
That is, she will reflect His divine attributes and holy nature.
She will be at His side to reign with the King of glory. All
Heaven now awaits the emergence of a company who will
make themselves ready, without spot or wrinkle, through the
impartation of the Holy Spirit.

This is a much loftier mandate and revelatory vision than
any experienced before. The kingdoms of this world are not
conquered without the process of refining and grooming.
Many Christians have been for quite some time in the phase of
expecting to reach maturity and to become able to carry significant spiritual authority.

# JUSTICE
### *and the*
# CLOUD *of*
# WITNESSES

CHAPTER

5

# DIVINE JUSTICE

Among the visions given to Daniel, the panorama of the Ancient of Days is truly extraordinary. Like the apostle John in Revelation 1, Daniel was given a view of God's administration of justice. Daniel saw Almighty God take His position in the courtroom of Heaven to render justice.

> I kept looking
> Until thrones were set up,
> And the Ancient of Days took His seat;
> His vesture was like white snow
> And the hair of His head like pure wool.
> His throne was ablaze with flames,
> Its wheels were a burning fire.
> A river of fire was flowing
> And coming out from before Him;

Thousands upon thousands were attending Him,
And myriads upon myriads were standing before Him;
The court sat,
And the books were opened.

—Daniel 7:9–10

The flaming eyes of the Judge have seen and recorded every action of humanity. All things are open and laid bare before the eyes of Him with whom we must give an account (Hebrews 4:13). The books of Heaven are going to be read and restitution offered for injustices committed against God's covenant people.

The enemy has battled the saints of God for millennia and seemingly prevailed. Nevertheless, God, as the Righteous Judge, will render a final verdict on behalf of the saints. But, until the time of justice arrives, the armies of darkness will venture to persecute, plunder, and murder many of the saints. Daniel recorded:

I kept looking, and that horn was waging war with the saints and overpowering them until the Ancient of Days came and judgment was passed in favor of the saints of the Highest One, and the time arrived when the saints took possession of the kingdom.

—Daniel 7:21–22

The revelation of divine justice, released to empower God's people and to subdue His enemies, will happen on this side of eternity. In this season we will taste the Kingdom power of the age to come. The Head will come to the body and impart the virtue of the overcoming King.

The fullness of the Kingdom will emerge after the things mentioned in the Book of Revelation have come to pass. However, we are promised a taste of that realm; we see it when believers over-come all odds and sit with Jesus on His throne. Those Kingdom saints demonstrate the virtue of the age to come.

The revelation of the Kingdom is directly tied to the unveiling of divine justice. The throne seen by Daniel and John bespeaks God's dominion and kingly authority—attributes that are integrally woven into the administration of justice. As the prophet Isaiah foresaw, the Lord's throne will be established in mercy and loving-kindness. The One who sits upon it will demonstrate truth and faithfulness in the restored Tabernacle of David. He will justly judge and swiftly execute righteousness in the earth (Isaiah 16:5).

## Tabernacle of David

The Bible clearly connects the restoration of the Tabernacle of David, prophesied through Amos, to the unveiling of the Lord's dominion and kingship.

When Paul and Barnabas returned from their successful first missionary journey, the disciples pondered their dilemma over Gentile converts. The apostles had the unexpected task of dealing with Gentiles who embraced the covenant blessings originally intended for the seed of Abraham. The Holy Spirit worked with these Gentile Christians in the same way that He did with Peter and the other apostles who walked with Jesus during His earthly ministry. The truth had been evidenced among them through miracles, signs, and wonders and had led to a bountiful harvest among the Gentiles.

After much discussion, James, led by the spirit of wisdom, finally addressed the assembly. He quoted Amos 9 and applied the prophetic promise of a restored Tabernacle of David to a Gentile people separated for the Lord and identified by His name. The apostle established spiritual relevance, saying:

Simeon has related how God first concerned Himself about taking from among the Gentiles a people for His name. With this the words of the Prophets agree, just as it is written:

'AFTER THESE THINGS I WILL RETURN,
AND I WILL REBUILD THE TABERNACLE OF
    DAVID WHICH HAS FALLEN,
AND I WILL REBUILD ITS RUINS,
AND I WILL RESTORE IT,
SO THAT THE REST OF MANKIND MAY SEEK
    THE LORD,
AND ALL THE GENTILES WHO ARE CALLED
    BY MY NAME,'
SAYS THE LORD, WHO MAKES THESE THINGS
    KNOWN FROM LONG AGO.

—Acts 15:14–17

The early apostles were dealing with an unprecedented application of the Scriptures. The promise of God, through the prophets of previous generations, was for restoration. Likewise, in this generation, we will deal with many unprecedented truths being applied and restored. Our only parameters for proper biblical application will be the words of Scripture and the Holy Spirit illuminating them.

The apostle James proclaimed a truth that has not yet been fully attained. No generation has witnessed the full restoration of the Tabernacle of David. We have yet to see the throne of Heaven and a demonstration of the Lord's justice in the earth. However, James's word must be fulfilled, and we are privileged to live in the day that will experience that notable achievement.

The day in which we now live can appropriately be called

the Laodicean age. From Greek, *Laodicea* means "justice of the people" or "people's rights." Sadly, this is a far cry from the justice of God. While the spirit of this world declares human rights first, Heaven declares divine justice and the biblical rights of God. A great confrontation between these two spirits is under way.

It is impossible for justice to be rendered by mere human hands; the heart of humanity is exceedingly evil. The Laodicean church age completely counters the justice the Lord desires to show His people. God overflows with equity, impartiality, and truth. However, there is an absence of true fairness in the heart of humanity, except when it is imparted by the Holy Spirit. Almighty God is perfect in His justice, while the god of this world is the epitome of injustice.

*We have yet to see the throne of Heaven and a demonstration of the Lord's justice in the earth. However, James's word must be fulfilled, and we are privileged to live in the day that will experience that notable achievement.*

God's justice should considerably encourage the believer in Jesus Christ. The Bible plainly outlines His attributes of purity and righteousness. Those who have been joined to Him and share in His righteousness have nothing to fear from His expression of justice. Actually, divine justice is a key mystery of the Kingdom and will launch the bride of Christ into the greatest harvest of souls ever witnessed in human history. God's justice rewards faithfulness but requires recompense for injustices committed against Him and His people.

Many of the apocalyptic and terrifying depictions of the last days stem from the side of the justice coin that judges unrighteousness. Fortunately divine justice is like a two-edged sword—one side of which is to be explored and embraced by the bride of Christ. The other is a harsh discipline on sin and violations of His word and nature. This is not a time to be separated from God; as one of my friends often says, "If you get in trouble, run to God—not from Him."

## The Ministry of Justice

Scripture affirms that righteousness and justice are the foundations of the Lord's throne. These dual attributes are the essence of His Kingdom and will be greatly emphasized during these pivotal days.

We have not fully embraced the justice of Heaven because we do not understand its absolute application. However, the Lord's justice will unleash an end-time army of believers equipped with the resources of Heaven. When He reveals Himself as the Just Judge, a verdict will be rendered in favor of the saints. All valuable callings, anointings, commissions, and gifts entrusted to God's people throughout the ages will be restored and redeemed.

A.W. Tozer wrote in *The Knowledge of the Holy* about heavenly justice:

> It is sometimes said, "Justice requires God to do this," referring to some act we know He will perform. This is an error of thinking as well as of speaking, for it postulates a principle of justice outside of God which compels Him to act in a certain way. Of course there is no such principle. If there were it would be superior to God, for only a superior power can compel obedience. The truth is that there is not and can never be anything outside of the nature of God which can move Him in the least degree. All God's reasons come from within His uncreated being.

Nothing has entered the being of God from eternity, nothing has been removed, and nothing has been changed. God is His own self-existent principle of moral equity, and when He sentences evil men or rewards the righteous, He simply acts like Himself from within, uninfluenced by anything that is not Himself (pages 93–94).

Divine justice renders blessings on behalf of the righteous and judgment upon unrighteousness. Justice restores what has been stolen and compensates the victim when the thief has been captured.

Men do not despise a thief if he steals
To satisfy himself when he is hungry;
But when he is found, he must repay sevenfold . . .
—Proverbs 6:30–31

Almost every believer can testify that he or she has been stolen from. For many, their children and family members have been inflicted with illnesses and hardships. Others have had finances devoured. Much of the spiritual inheritance entrusted to God's people has been unlawfully taken. Precious ministry gifts and spiritual anointings have been lost through incursions of demonic "bandits."

For millennia, history has recorded the blatant activity of the thief and his vile plans and strategies against God's people. The horn of the enemy has been lifted up against the covenant people of Heaven. He has used tactics of destruction employing weapons that include sickness, disease, death, financial calamity, corrupt political and civil authorities, abortion, drug and alcohol addictions, sin, depression, and accidents, to name just a few.

The annals of history are saturated with innumerable accounts of wrongful persecutions, torture, and martyrdoms of saintly men and women.

Commentaries and journals have recorded the lives of valiant faithful men and women who sacrificially gave themselves to be butchered at the hands of religious zealots. Many were wrongfully tortured and executed in the name of religion; in fact, they were martyrs for Christ.

Everything has taken place under the all-seeing eye of God, and He has promised to restore all that our adversary has ruined. His just nature requires it both in this life and the one to come. Clearly these saints have received a martyr's reward in eternity. They have also sown spiritual seeds that will result in God giving the most outstanding deposit of grace ever demonstrated.

**I Will Restore**

Over the past year the Lord has spoken to me about "the economy of Heaven." This at first seemed like an unusual expression. However, as the Holy Spirit began to teach me about the issues of spiritual justice, I discovered how the Lord's economy functions and why He allows certain things to happen. His economy will not allow any of His impartation and heavenly endowments to be lost forever; He will recover and amplify everything the enemy has attempted to devour and destroy.

The Joel 2:25 promise of restoration is one of the paramount passages of this day. God's pledges:

> So I will restore to you the years that the
> swarming locust has eaten,
> The crawling locust,
> The consuming locust,
> And the chewing locust,

My great army which I sent among you.
You shall eat in plenty and be satisfied,
And praise the name of the LORD your God,
Who has dealt wondrously with you;
And My people shall never be put to shame.

—Joel 2:25–26

For thousands of years God's children have been martyred, persecuted, desecrated, and plundered. But the justice of Heaven will decree that all be fully restored and compensated. Furthermore, this generation has experienced corruption on a scale rarely seen in history. Poverty, famine, murder, rape, and other tragedies have so infiltrated our society that we have become numb to them. Tragic daily news reports have become so commonplace that they rarely capture people's attention. Darkness has become exceedingly dark. Nonetheless, the promise of Heaven is that there shall be light in the evening time.

On a personal level this truth should reassure and free every Christian who has endured difficulty and hardship. We have often wondered why the enemy seems to be able to steal our joy, peace, health, and, in some cases, our youth. It is not because the Lord was unconcerned for us—quite the contrary! Instead, God desires to bless us and use us in profound ways and bring glory to His name. Divine justice will render recompense.

### Revelation of Jesus, the Just Judge

Both Daniel and John were given phenomenal revelatory encounters with the just Judge. His judgments are perfect, and His ways far surpass the scrutiny of human understanding. His justice embodies a promise for the welfare of His people and the unfolding of His Kingdom on earth. His mysterious justice unlocks the virtue of Heaven.

The apostle John's account described several different aspects of God's justice in the book of Revelation. He saw the Lord adorned in His royal attire, representing His authority.

### His Hair White like Snow

John's depiction of the Lord's hair—"white like snow"—symbolizes the supreme wisdom by which He judges the affairs of humanity. The people of Israel vividly remembered the glory once resident in their nation under the leadership of King Solomon. The heavenly impartation of wisdom given to this king is legendary; but now one greater than Solomon has come. Jesus, who is the source of all wisdom, will judge humanity according to the books of Heaven.

Both John and Daniel saw the purity of God's wisdom in His justice portrayed by hair white like snow. Revealed as the suffering Lamb, the overcoming King we will now see shall wage war and render justice upon His enemies (Revelation 19:11).

### His Eyes like a Flame of Fire

The penetrating and fiery eyes of Jesus the Just Judge have seen all that has taken place throughout history. Nothing has escaped His notice; even humanity's motives and thoughts resonate in Heaven.

The eyes of God have recorded every act of righteousness and every injustice on earth. Not one injustice will be left without restitution and restoration.

> For who has despised the day of small things? But these seven will be glad when they see the plumb line in the hand of Zerubbabel—these are the eyes of the LORD which range to and fro throughout the earth.
> —Zechariah 4:10

## Feet like Burnished Bronze

His burnished bronze feet represent His right to stand executing justice. Bronze is a very hard substance that has been tried by fire. The sinless, spotless Son of God endured the harshness of iniquity on behalf of all humanity. The fiery furnace of God's wrath against sin was heaped upon the Lord Jesus. He took it to the cross and won the right to release justice in the earth.

His feet will stand upon the land and sea and deliver justice in the human realm. Only He can carry the burden of this royal responsibility; only He has paid the great price for that redemption. Moses prophetically saw the Lord, in His glory, revealing the attributes of both mercy and justice. As the Lord passed before Moses, He declared His eternal qualities of compassion and grace. He is slow to anger and abounds in loving-kindness and truth. He extends mercy and forgiveness to thousands, pardoning iniquity, transgression and sin. But by no means does He leave the guilt of sin unpunished.

If iniquity has been released through repentance to the Lord Jesus, no judgment for sin remains. Justice then bestows blessings, favor, and grace to the righteous.

## The Sound of Many Waters

Waters often symbolically point to the multitudes of peoples and nations. In their midst, His voice is the voice of ultimate authority and power. Throughout the ages a prophetic message has been entrusted to every generation through messengers of Heaven. An allotted portion of heavenly manna has been deposited in every juncture of Church history.

Daniel, in his prayer of repentance, acknowledged that the people of his day did not obey the voice of the Lord presented to them through the prophets. He wrote:

Nor have we obeyed the voice of the LORD our God,
to walk in His teachings which He set before us
through His servants the prophets.

—Daniel 9:10

When the day of justice arrives, every voice that has declared the revelation of God to his or her generation will sound as one. That voice will be the voice of the Holy Spirit rendering justice.

### Seven Stars

The Holy Spirit uses humans to articulate His voice. The seven stars seen by John are the ambassadors of Heaven who carried and imparted the revelation of Jesus to their generations. Scriptures indicate that the seven stars were God's messengers.

*Ultimately this upcoming generation will comprise a company of messengers who not only impart a truth but actually embody the Truth. That is our promise and legacy.*

The apostle Paul was a messenger and voice to the early Church. He worked in cooperation with the Holy Spirit and the host of Heaven. The message was oftentimes communicated to him and the apostle John through spiritual beings who embodied the revelation of God. That pattern has continued throughout Church history and will be emphasized in this day.

Martin Luther was a messenger to his day, restoring the truth that the just shall live by faith. The progressive recovery of lost heritage continued through the messengers of the next generation, including John Wesley, George Whitefield, John Knox, and many others.

Similarly the twentieth century also produced key prophetic voices who were pioneers burning with a message of truth. The ministry of healing was restored to the corporate body along with the baptism of the Holy Spirit, as was witnessed at Azusa Street. Ultimately this upcoming generation will comprise a company of messengers who not only impart a truth but actually embody the Truth. That is our promise and legacy.

## Two-Edged Sword

The living Word is quick and powerful and sharper than a two-edged sword. Only the Lord can separate spirit from soul. He is the one who discerns the thoughts and intentions of our hearts. The Lord Jesus has the unique ability to examine and weigh our motives to determine if we are capable of carrying the authority of Heaven to our generation. It is His intent and desire to live in and among His people; He seeks to bring revelation of Himself and His Word. The Book of Revelation, declaring that Jesus is faithful and true, records that He will return on a white horse. Embroidered on His garment will be the depiction of His person as the Word of God. The Word became flesh and dwelt among humanity. He once again desires to do the same through His Church.

## Face like the Sun

The Lord bears many holy attributes. While some people still see the Lord as a baby in a manger, He is now an awesome, victorious, overcoming King. Great is His power and authority to be administered!

The Son of Righteousness will arise with healing in His wings and bring a fresh revelation of His nature to the earth. The residue of glory resting on Moses after his face-to-face encounters with God overwhelmed the people of Israel. He was forced to cover his face because of the tangible impartation of heavenly virtue he carried. Imagine what could happen in this generation! Christ in us—the hope of glory—this endowment will come to those who view Him with an unveiled face.

## Our Day of Justice

The apostle John was caught up in the Spirit and shown a revelation of the Lord Jesus, steeped in justice. The Lord has provided several supernatural signposts throughout the past decades to mark our place in biblical history. We can confidently approach the end-time promises received by John with faith and assurance of their application to the present hour in which we are living. Divine justice is a key to the Kingdom that will unlock great blessings and resources for the bride of Christ.

CHAPTER

6

# PLUNDERING
## *the* ENEMY CAMP

When I shared a message of divine justice at a conference in Amarillo, Texas, a minister from Dallas responded with a wonderful affirmation. At the conclusion of the service, a distinguished–looking, elderly gentleman approached and asked if we could have a brief conversation. Frankly my first reaction was to think he might have had difficulty with my message. However, as soon as he began to speak, I sensed the anointing and sincerity of the Holy Spirit in him. I could readily discern that he appreciated the message.

He began by sharing a recent supernatural experience where he was caught up into a heavenly place in much the same fashion described by Paul in 2 Corinthians 12:2–4. He was taken in the spirit to a large room the size of a football field. He felt it had the atmosphere and appearance of a courtroom. He said the experience was so real, it was as fresh in his memory as something that had happened in the natural realm.

The courtroom was empty, except for the Lord Jesus, who was seated in an elevated position as the divine judge. This man was the only one standing before the judge's seat.

The Lord asked him, "Do you believe that I allow My people to be plundered?" This brother thought for a moment and remembered the biblical stories of David and Job. He said he did believe that, on occasion, the Lord allowed His people to be plundered for a good cause.

"My son, do you believe I will allow the enemy to plunder you to the point of death?" the Lord asked him.

"No, Lord," the man replied. "I believe You release protection over the lives of Your people." At that the doors to the courtroom burst open, and Satan himself abruptly marched before the Lord.

*When the people of God discover the reality of the Almighty's divine justice and ask Him to release divine restoration, we will begin to plunder the enemy's camp and bring every lost gift back to the Church.*

"I demand the right to plunder this man," Satan said to Jesus.

Surprisingly Jesus granted permission for Satan's unholy intrusion into the life of this man. Needless to say, the man was not happy that permission was given for the adversary to pillage his life. But the Lord told Satan: "I will grant you permission to plunder his life, but it is going to cost you."

"I have plundered Your people for thousands of years, and it hasn't cost me very much at all," Satan replied.

At that abrasive statement the Lord turned to the man. "When My people learn to come before Me and request justice, then they will plunder the enemy's camp," He said.

I was stunned by the divine affirmation provided by this brother. At the time he shared his experience, I had not talked with anyone else who had encountered this realm of Heaven and brought a message like the one I was delivering. I was very thankful to the Lord for having this man in the meeting to provide confirmation and encouragement to further reveal this end-time mystery.

When the people of God discover the reality of the Almighty's divine justice and ask Him to release divine restoration, we will begin to plunder the enemy's camp and bring every lost gift back to the Church.

## Overcoming Self-Pity

Part of our calling is to discover these realms of heavenly justice and to do what is necessary to plunder the enemy's camp. We are called to restore the gifts and inheritances of the saints. The economy of Heaven will demand the return of all that has been stolen by the enemy. When we come to the Lord's court to petition for justice, Jesus will hear and respond. The day has arrived for the revelation of His throne and its qualities of righteousness and justice.

Satan knows this and is already working to nullify God's grace and preempt His administration of justice. One of the accuser's favorite tactics to stop our promised recovery is to sow seeds of self-pity within the souls of men and women.

Many Christians look back on the difficulties of life and develop an unhealthy retrospective disposition. Out of this, self-pity can emerge if it is not properly dealt with at the cross. Self-pity is one of the most obvious weapons in the arsenal employed against Christians. This snare paves the way for grief, shame, and unbelief. It is a stronghold used by the adversary to stop God from fully using us. Self-pity is a demonic power that can lock people in a stifling dungeon of darkness. The Lord Jesus said:

> Therefore take heed that the light which is in you is not darkness. If then your whole body is full of light, having no part dark, the whole body will be full of light, as when the bright shining of a lamp gives you light.
> —Luke 11:35–36, NKJV

In the spiritual realm, characteristics and emotions of a fallen nature take on a vibrant life of their own. When confronted with difficulty and hardships from our past, we can emerge from them either healthier or handicapped. If we are overcome by self-pity, we never allow the spiritual principles of restoration and recompense to be set in motion. When we have a fully submitted will, the spiritual dynamics activated on our behalf open the door for spiritual fruitfulness. The choice is ours.

With the proper decisions the Lord will give us beauty for ashes and the oil of joy for mourning. He will give us the garment of praise in exchange for the spirit of heaviness. This apparel is defined as spiritual raiment that clothes us in light. This light can keep us free from the darkness working to consume us.

We are called to be engaged, encompassed, and enveloped by heavenly provision. Let us tangibly embrace this realm of the spirit and clothe ourselves with heavenly garments; otherwise we allow ourselves to be overcome by darkness, discouragement, and depression and this limits, or even nullifies, the complete apportionment of grace we appropriate by the blood of Christ.

## Plundering the Enemy's Camp

Several years ago my friend Bob Jones had an important prophetic experience. It is not uncommon for Bob to have angelic visitations and revelatory encounters in which he is taken into the heavenly realm. During these times, he has seen the plans and strategies of the Lord. Like the prophet Elisha, Bob is also often allowed to spy into demonic traps and snares orchestrated against God's people and to offer counterstrategies of prayer and intercession. He is one of the few people I would acknowledge as truly occupying the office of a mature prophet of the Lord.

In this specific experience the Lord Himself appeared and told Bob that they were about to go into the "trophy room" of Satan to retrieve something of significant spiritual value that belonged to the Body of Christ. Only the Lord can safely take someone into a place identified as the treasury of Satan. It is a spiritual domain in the heavenly places in which our adversary harnesses the valuable gifts and spiritual endowments he has successfully stolen from the Body of Christ. These anointings must be reclaimed.

*Throughout millennia every expression of spiritual outpouring has been accompanied by allotments of spiritual talents, displays of power, and valuable gifts; the enemy has targeted these most in his sinister schemes.*

Throughout Judeo-Christian history we have witnessed many wonderful gifts, ministries, and anointings for spiritual impartation. Unfortunately most have been ensnared by the enemy; they have been captured in the same way that the serpent seized the authority once delegated to Adam. The deception, and subsequent sin of Adam and Eve, caused a breach that allowed dominion to be illegitimately usurped by Satan. Throughout millennia every expression of spiritual outpouring has been accompanied by allotments of spiritual talents, displays of power, and valuable gifts; the enemy has targeted these most in his sinister schemes.

These rich heritages must be retrieved in this generation. As the Lord took Bob into this place, he saw such valuable spiritual items as "the tambourine of Miriam" and the "harp of David." Satan has stolen "mantles of evangelism" and "robes of revivalists" meant for the Body of Christ that now await righteous individuals to reacquire and impart them to a needy generation. In addition, there are creative arts and musical gifts that have only been partially discovered and used in this world. They are now held in heavenly places, but a complete release in the earth for the glory of the Kingdom will come.

Many musicians and artists have become cultural icons through abilities and talents given to them by God. The enemy, however, clouded their minds and took the precious gifts originally intended for the Body of Christ. These can now be retrieved and reintroduced.

Many of these natural and spiritual attributes were hijacked from God's people through elaborate plots, schemes, and devices of the adversary—he ensnared the people who carried them. Others were simply lost because God shares His glory with no one. King Uzziah touched the Ark of the Covenant, and it cost him his life. The Lord greatly helped Uzziah until his heart became rotted with pride. Human flesh cannot be allowed to touch God's glory. When it does, precious wine is lost . . . along with the wineskin.

### Banner of Holiness

As Bob surveyed the enemy treasury with the Lord, he knew the mission was to repossess something incredibly valuable for the Body of Christ. In fact, it was a prized possession of Satan's and a figure that was the centerpiece of his "trophy room."

Although much of Satan's highly valued loot filled this room, the Lord intended to retrieve only one object of restoration on this mission. This item is the vital spiritual heritage that provides a foundation for all other impartations of power and authority: It is our calling and admonition to live in a purified state before Him.

Shortly after entering this foreboding domain, the Lord escorted Bob to a table covered with a black velvetlike material. There Bob saw the banner God intended to retrieve and deliver back to the Church. This banner, so cherished by the enemy, was the banner of "holiness." Satan has, for many years, convinced the Body of Christ that it is impossible to live in purity and holiness.

The centerpiece of Satan's trophy room was an essential spiritual truth represented on a white banner bordered with blue material. The inscription on the standard was written with golden Hebrew letters that said:

"You shall be holy, for I the LORD your God am holy."
—Leviticus 19:2

Somehow the enemy had stolen the message of holiness from the Church; now the Lord intended to restore this truth to His people. Bob seized the banner and followed the Lord out of that dark domain.

### The Divine Nature
The Bible states that we have precious and magnificent promises by which we can become partakers of the divine nature and escape the corruption of this world (2 Peter 1:4). That certainty is a heritage that once belonged to us but now is part of a desolate inheritance about to be restored. A generation expe-

riencing the complete sanctification of spirit, soul, and body and walking before God in harmony is about to be loosed. It will be a company of overcomers who will be holy as He is holy. They will not manage this through their own strength but through God's loving-kindness and grace.

This company will become one with Jesus, even as He was one with the Father. Enoch saw this generation in his prophetic revelations; his words were later affirmed by Jude 14-15. The Lord Jesus is coming with holy ones who share His nature and live free of the corruption of this world.

When Bob took the banner from the table, "all hell broke loose," he says. The enemy was furious that the grace to manifest this truth had come. Immediately, the Lord took Bob from Satan's trophy room into the refuge of the "sheep gate" described in John 10.

Like the message of justification by faith restored through Martin Luther, this edict of holiness is being retrieved and imparted back to God's people. Luther reinstated a lost birthright to the Body of Christ; the restoration of desolate heritages continues today.

Since Bob's experience more has been written and preached on the message of holiness than in many years prior.

### Now Is the Time

Another sister in the Lord told of a similar experience in Satan's trophy room. She was similarly taken there; she and Jesus went to retrieve an embroidered robe representing the nature and character of Christ (Colossians 3:12–14). The enemy has tried to cheat us out of the rich heritage provided by Christ's redemption and the garments of salvation and righteousness He purchased on our behalf.

The time has now come for the Body of Christ to arise in

faith and power to plunder the enemy's camp and secure our rich heritage. Mantles of healing and deliverance, as well as garments of salvation, can be captured and displayed in this hour. Like our spiritual predecessors, we must please the Lord and gain the testimony of overcomers in order to be endowed with the heavenly virtue that is our high calling and lofty mandate.

## Reaping Spiritual Benefits

The apostle Paul understood the principle of justice and restoration. He considered the persecution and hardship he endured to be simply light and momentary afflictions. He recognized the authority of divine justice and knew that the hardships he endured only created a far greater eternal weight of glory for him. His tribulations produced a spiritual reward described as transcendent glory and blessings. The reward, though, came in the form of spiritual benefits that were the fruit of the unseen world (2 Corinthians 4:17–18).

*The Bible teaches us that we should no longer emphasize what is seen but instead focus on what is unseen. The visible is temporary and fleeting; the invisible is everlasting.*

The Bible teaches us that we should no longer emphasize what is seen but instead focus on what is unseen. The visible is temporary and fleeting; the invisible is everlasting. Though our difficulties in life may have resulted in financial loss, personal misfortunes, and physical and emotional suffering, they will render a spiritual return of favor and grace.

The Lord created a generation to discover and explore the realms of justice. He foresaw a company who would come before His court to request the unveiling of equity for all the adversary had stolen. Exploitation and hardship endured in youth, when properly submitted to the Lord and His grace, can result in tremendous outpourings of favor and restitution for the sake of the Kingdom. He has promised He would restore *all* that the enemy has devoured.

Perhaps someone lost a parent and suffered immensely because of the ordeals the family went through. Heaven's justice can bring recompense for those difficult years. The devil took full advantage of his opportunity to plunder the life of Job. In the end, however, the enemy's rampage released the Lord to extend even greater measures of His goodness and favor upon that notable patriarch and his family.

We could list thousands of ways Satan has attempted to steal from a generation of destiny. The principle remains the same, regardless of the specific circumstance: The Lord Jesus is a just God, and the world is about to witness the unfolding of His royal attributes and kingly authority. He is about to unleash an unprecedented demonstration of spiritual justice.

### Retrieving a Mantle of Evangelism

On Yom Kippur 2002, the Lord gave me a vision. I found myself in a large, very deep body of water. The water was crystal clear and a perfect temperature. Simply being in the water was one of the most pleasurable sensations I have ever had. However, without realizing it, I was being drawn deeper and deeper into the water until the surface could barely be seen. Yet the bottom was undetectable.

At this point a certain reverential awe and fearfulness began to emerge in me. As Scriptures point out, the Lord dwells in deep darkness. In this place, one is completely vulnerable and at the mercy of God. It was both exhilarating and terrifying. It is a place where a human meets with God without pretense or disguise. I remained at that depth for a few contemplative moments until I felt the need to return to the surface. I wasn't out of breath, though, for it was as natural to breathe in this water as it is to breathe in a cool breeze along the shore of the Gulf of Mexico.

As I began to make my way back toward the surface, I was drawn to an underwater rock ledge. There I discovered a fishing lure resting in one of the crevices. I could tell it had once been a very productive lure, but the line had been broken, and the lure had been lost. This lure represented an evangelistic mantle that had been worn with considerable success; it had drawn many sinners to Christ and the Kingdom of Heaven. Unfortunately, the carrier of the anointing had been ensnared in a trap of the enemy and had lost the "lure."

I contemplated seizing the lure and taking it back, but I was forbidden by the Holy Spirit to touch it. Instead I was instructed to return to the surface and bring a man back to the location of the lure; only he could retrieve and restore it.

Later I was told the lure specifically represented a powerful evangelistic mantle worn previously by someone else. Unfortunately, the lure, or mantle, had been lost when the line had been broken, severing the flow of grace essential for that commission. The Lord was now preparing to recapture it. That gift would rest upon someone—or a company of people—who have discovered God in deep darkness. Their character and nature are being groomed by Him.

The enemy thought the anointing had been lost forever in the depths of the water. However, the Lord caused it to rest upon a ledge so it could be reassigned. This symbolic lure is representative of the mantles of evangelism that have been stolen by the evil one and held in heavenly places until they could be restored. The ministry of God's justice will see to that.

# 7

# THE ECONOMY of HEAVEN

I started pondering this justice message when Steve Kinney, a good friend of mine, passed away at the age of thirty-eight. Steve had been the faithful pastor of a church in Kodiak, Alaska. He left behind a precious wife, two daughters, and many friends.

It was common for Steve and me to have lengthy phone conversations several times a week. In them we shared spiritual insight and personal expectancy for God to do mighty things. He would often relate his deep desire to see the presence of God visit Alaska as a spiritual gate to the west. He devoted himself to that end.

In one summer the Lord sent several notable international ministries to the little church in Kodiak. I believe this represents a sign of the esteem Steve held with the Lord. There was no reason in the natural for these ministries to be sent to this little fishing community; the only explanation was the favor of God. Steve had somehow obtained a testimony from God and became the friend of Jesus.

In September 2002 Wanda and I received the shocking news that Steve had collapsed and died. Needless to say, I asked the Lord how such a thing could happen to one of His faithful servants. This seemed like a clear intrusion from the adversary. There was no blatant sin or corruption—only a faithful pastor and friend who longed to see revival come to Alaska and this nation.

At the time of Steve's death, Wanda and I were involved in a prophetic conference with Bobby Connor and Bob Jones in Asheville, North Carolina. We had also committed to another conference in Greensboro. Because of these dates, we were not able to speak at the initial funeral service held in Kodiak just after Steve passed away; however, we were able to attend a memorial service for him a few days later.

## Justice and the Cloud of Witnesses

It was at the conference in Greensboro that the Lord began my journey of understanding concerning the divine administration of justice and its relationship to the "cloud of witnesses."

During the conference my friend Wade Taylor shared his testimony. In it he told how the Lord had blessed him with three very notable men of faith and power as mentors. One was Walter Beuttler.

Wade told how Beuttler had found intimacy with the Lord. He had developed a close personal friendship with Jesus and became an imitation of the Lord's nature and character; he had entered the Lord's rest. This sincere and humble man would quietly stand before people and share his testimony of intimacy. His words and heart captured the attention of every person in a room. Not only that, the Lord would also touch his meetings with a remarkable display of His presence and power. He validated Beuttler's message. Never did he claim to be a great preacher—he was just a friend of God.

On one specific occasion in 1951 Beuttler committed himself to a forty-eight-hour session of prayer and fasting. At the end of the two days he received a visitation from the Lord Jesus that lasted for four hours. During that time the Lord carried this faithful man through the Bible and imparted an experiential reality of "knowing God." Such were the encounters he had with the Lord.

*How could such a thing occur to a righteous man of God walking in awesome levels of friendship and fellowship with the Divine?*

So striking was Beuttler's ministry that his calendar was filled five years in advance with appointments and meetings around the world. His personal relationship with the Lord and his ministry were flourishing. Yet at the height of it all Beuttler was smitten with cancer and died at a relatively young age.

How could such a thing occur to a righteous man of God walking in awesome levels of friendship and fellowship with the Divine? That was the very question Wade Taylor asked the Lord.

When Wade publicly shared the response he received from God, I knew it was also the answer to my questions about Steve.

"I have more need of him here than you do there," the Lord said of Wade's mentor.

Somehow, there was a greater need for Walter Beuttler in Heaven than on the earth. This was strangely true despite the awesome international ministry entrusted to him. There was a role and responsibility in Heaven that would somehow impact the end-time plan of God and the harvest of the ages.

**The Economy of Heaven**

As Wade shared his story of Walter Beuttler, the Holy Spirit outlined for me how the economy of Heaven operates—in fact, this was the first time I had heard the phrase "economy of Heaven" from the Lord. The Bible says that a sevenfold restoration must be exacted when a thief has been captured. When the enemy comes in to steal, kill, and destroy through violent invasion, it paves the way for amplified restoration and restitution.

This spiritual principle only operates when there has been no obvious open door given to the enemy through sin, rebellion, or blatant disobedience. This deliberate enemy intrusion sets in motion the justice of God and requires a release of grace to balance the scales. When accomplished, the restoration is multiplied according to the mandates of Scripture.

> Men do not despise a thief if he steals
> To satisfy himself when he is hungry;
> But when he is found, he must repay sevenfold . . . .
> —Proverbs 6:30–31

Seven is a number symbolically identified with "completion or perfection." The Bible is promising a complete repayment. There may literally be a sevenfold return for those things lost. Furthermore the Bible also portrays principles of sowing and reaping with potential harvests of thirty, sixty, and hundredfold returns. This all depends upon the character and faithfulness of the laborers.

Walter Beuttler was living a life of purity and consecration. The cancer imposed upon his body was an attack by the enemy. Therefore when justice is rendered, the Lord is now empowered to restore not just the anointing that rested upon Walter Beuttler's life but a sevenfold amplification of it. That is the economy of Heaven. When one measure of anointing is stolen, the Lord is warranted to give a multiplied increase.

The enemy violated this brother in an illegal way and invaded his life with disease. That was an unjust intrusion. He did nothing to expose himself. If a man were to smoke five packs of cigarettes a day and then be afflicted with lung cancer, he cannot necessarily claim it was an invasion of the thief. More appropriately, it is the fruit of decisions and acts of the human will. Similarly people who drink alcohol on a daily basis for many years and develop liver damage could be reaping what has been sown rather than suffering from an unjust violation.

In the case of Walter Beuttler no such open door or opportunity was granted through rebellion or a negligent act of self-will. Instead it was the evil one's intent to steal the powerful ministry and anointing entrusted to this loyal saint. According to the economy of Heaven, when the thief is captured, the Lord is justified to release back to the earth seven people like Walter Beuttler.

### The Wisdom of Heaven

The wicked one has worked seemingly successfully to plunder the people of God throughout the millennia. However, as with the crucifixion of our Lord, he does not understand God's mysterious ways. According to the apostle Paul, the rulers of this age did not perceive or recognize the wisdom of Heaven. If they had, they would not have crucified the Lord of glory (1 Corinthians 2:8).

Likewise it has seemed that the enemy has been able to pillage God's gifts given to His people. But his actions have only stored up spiritual provision the Lord can now justifiably release into a generation of destiny. That is why Hebrews 11:39–12:1 affirms that the "cloud of witnesses" would not be made perfect apart from us. Those who sow and those who reap will rejoice together! Spiritual deposits have been sown, and we will be the beneficiaries who reap them through the justice of Heaven.

Walter Beuttler greatly impacted the realm of the spirit by teaching people what a living relationship with God was like. He was a great threat to Satan and the kingdom of darkness. Though his life was wrongfully ended, we can now justifiably expect many more to emerge with the anointing and authority that rested upon this man. What the enemy intended for evil, God will use for good.

> *During the Dark Ages, countless thousands died because of their unwillingness to bow their knee to religious falsehood or someone assuming the position of Christ on the earth.*

When he died, Beuttler entered the "cloud of witnesses." However, he will continue to reap a bountiful harvest from every impartation the Lord is now able to release through His justice. His life was like a spiritual seed planted to acquire a more substantial reward. It was not because of any virtue resident in Beuttler, but because of the Holy Spirit he carried.

The same principle is true throughout history involving every saint of God whose life was wrongfully ended. During the Dark Ages, countless thousands died because of their unwillingness to bow their knee to religious falsehood or someone assuming the position of Christ on the earth. The administration of the Lord's justice will allow amplified blessings to be delegated to God's people in response to their sacrifice.

**Freedom from Grief**
Each time I have shared this justice message publicly, the Lord

has released His grace to bring freedom to those suffering in the prison of grief. Many are captured and overwhelmed by the loss of loved ones, but the eternal truth of the Lord's justice will set them free. The realization that those precious to them will reap an eternal harvest is greatly comforting and liberating. Their sacrifice was not without a cause.

This truth has produced great peace and expectancy for our family personally. In 1995 we buried my younger brother; he was just thirty-two. For eighteen months Wanda and I had continually fasted and prayed for the healing of his terminal illness. Finally, after he had wasted away to eighty-seven pounds, the Lord visited me and told me I had to release my brother to Heaven.

At first, I thought about the many hours of prayer and fasting we had done for his healing. The Lord responded by assuring me that not one moment of prayer and fasting would be lost. If I would sow my brother as a seed and allow Him to take my brother to Heaven, God promised we would reap a harvest of healing. Not only that, but my brother would share in the eternal fruit God would receive because of my brother's life being sown. That truth broke my bonds of grief and released spiritual freedom.

## The All-Seeing Eye of God

Nothing transpires on the earth without the all-seeing eye of God taking notice. Clearly the enemy could not have gained an advantage over my friend Steve, Walter Beuttler, nor the saints throughout the ages if it had not been allowed by the Father. Yet there is a higher form of wisdom we must trust. We must view things from Heaven's perspective in order to experience God's provision for this notable day.

The devoted saints of history held an incredible zeal for God and willingness to live sacrificially. Very few today, particularly in the Western Church, can fully appreciate the level of conse-cration and devotion these ancestors exemplified. Yet though we are perhaps the least deserving generation of any, we will never-theless be the beneficiaries of the most stupendous deposits of divine grace ever displayed on the earth. That is why the cap-stone comes with shouts of grace-grace—this is an expression of multiplied levels of divine grace (Zechariah 4:7).

When we fully understand and embrace this multiplicative principle of God's justice, we will be compensated for all that has been stolen throughout history.

### The Friends of God

On Yom Kippur 2002 while waiting on the Lord, God told me about my friend Steve Kinney: "Steve became My friend," the Lord said. I was also given Hebrews 11:39–40 as a way to understand this concept better.

The Lord's statement spoke volumes to me. I suddenly knew that Steve's death related to God's justice and the restoration of all that has been stolen from the worthy saints, prophets, and patriarchs listed in Hebrews 11. This distinguished company of spiritual heroes—and others like them throughout history—were friends of God. A spiritual accounting will be exacted for Steve and all who have died in similar fashion.

Through this understanding I knew that my friend had somehow entered into an agreement with Heaven. He had become the Lord's friend and allowed himself to be sown as a spiritual seed, like many others, to see revival come to Alaska and to America.

CHAPTER

# 8

# THE CLOUD
## *of* WITNESSES

I believe that substantial insight into the "cloud of witnesses" is about to be given to the Body of Christ. Throughout history many faithful prophets and saints have prophetically seen the promises of God. They received divine approval for their faith but did not fully realize those promises in their day. Even so, the Bible highlights the strategy of God to see the fulfillment of the promises:

Therefore, since we have so great a cloud of witnesses surrounding us, let us also lay aside every encumbrance and the sin which so easily entangles us, and let us run with endurance the race that is set before us, fixing our eyes on Jesus, the author and perfecter of faith, who for the joy set before Him endured the cross, despising the shame, and has sat down at the right hand of the throne of God.

—Hebrews 12:1–2

Jesus has a divine strategy. According to Paul, God's dutiful saints will not come to perfection apart from a future generation of destiny. Furthermore, Scripture emphasizes that we are surrounded by a great cloud of witnesses who give testimony to God's faithfulness. They continue to carry the weight of divine promises and the burdens of His heart.

> *Those living in the end-time generation are challenged with the awesome privilege and great opportunity to inherit long foreseen promises.*

Those living in the end-time generation are challenged with the awesome privilege and great opportunity to inherit long foreseen promises. Mystically the prayers and sacrifices of our spiritual forefathers are somehow joined with us in the unveiling of God's grand finale.

## Those Who Testify

In the original Greek, the phrase *cloud of witnesses* is a judicial term and could more accurately be translated "cloud of testifiers." According to the translators, this phrase is taken from a courtroom setting. It is not about spectators but those involved in the trial. As in human courts of law, witnesses are called to testify, under oath, about the truth of what they have personally experienced. Individuals are not permitted to give hearsay or secondhand information. Only valid truth they have witnessed firsthand is allowed.

True apostolic leadership will be commissioned with a fourfold mandate like the one given to Paul. The Lord sent Ananias, one of His cherished friends, to release a prophetic commission to Paul, the newly converted Saul of Tarsus:

> A certain Ananias, a man who was devout by the standard of the Law, and well spoken of by all the Jews who lived there, came to me, and standing near said to me, "Brother Saul, receive your sight!" And at that very time I looked up at him. And he said, "The God of our fathers has appointed you to know His will and to see the Righteous One and to hear an utterance from His mouth. For you will be a witness for Him to all men of what you have seen and heard."
>
> —Acts 22:12-15

Paul was empowered with four privileges that exemplified his apostolic calling:

1. He was appointed to know God's will.
2. He saw the Righteous One.
3. He heard utterances from His lips.
4. He bore witness (testified) to what he saw and heard.

In our day, these attributes will separate true governmental qualities from those operating through a worldly spirit. Divinely anointed eyes and ears are essential in accomplishing this apostolic mandate and granting access to Heaven's revelatory realm. Through a spirit of revelation, God's will shall be apprehended and articulated by credible witnesses.

We will be shocked when we discover how closely the heavenly host observes us. They have won that right by investing in this day and gaining approval from Heaven for the faith they carried. They offer firsthand testimony of the prophetic purposes of Heaven.

All these, having obtained a good testimony through
faith, did not receive the promise, God having provided
something better for us, that they should not be made
perfect apart from us.

—Hebrews 11:39-40, NIV

Naturally Scripture provides parameters for this spiritual
dimension. In no way will the Bible permit spiritism or the
conjuring of individuals in the heavenly realm. Rather, the
Bible says that the Lord is the Captain of a host in Heaven; He
has ultimate authority over them.

Moses and Elijah were sent by the Father to encourage the
Lord Jesus in His earthly ministry. Likewise, in Revelation, the
apostle John spoke with someone in Heaven who identified
himself as one of the prophets.

## Unless a Grain of Wheat Dies
In John 12:24, a key spiritual principle is given to us:

Most assuredly, I say to you, unless a grain of wheat
falls into the ground and dies, it remains alone; but if
it dies, it produces much grain.

—John 12:24, NIV

This idea symbolically prophesied Jesus' sacrifice on the
cross; His life was a seed sown in order to reap a bountiful harvest. That same principle extends to those who carry the
deposit of Heaven in every generation.

Many notable saints, prophets, and friends of God carried
the testimony of Jesus to their generation. Countless millions
gave their lives for the sake of the Kingdom. Their spiritual
deposit will produce a lavish harvest through the justice of God.

Their blood was required because they were a part of Christ.

## A Prophetic Model

A prophetic model of this reality was also given in the Old Testament through the captivity of Israel. For four centuries the Israelites labored long and hard in Egypt under the harshest conditions imaginable. For many generations their slave labor empowered Egypt to prosper as the most dominant nation on the face of the earth. However, when the time came for their liberation, a single generation became the beneficiary of four hundred years of slavery.

The economy of Heaven and the justice of God ensured that Israel left Egypt with full compensation for their years of sacrificial labor and hardship. The Lord had promised that He would:

> ...judge the nation whom they will serve, and afterward they will come out with many possessions.
> —Genesis 15:14

According to the design of God, there was one generation who became the beneficiary of four hundred years of sacrifice, labor, and prayer. One generation of Israelites became the recipient of the promise of deliverance; the great wealth of Egypt accompanied their liberation. Those living in the day of salvation became the spiritual and natural beneficiaries of four hundred years of innocent blood shed. This paved the way for a great blessing, for:

> . . . the LORD had given the people favor in the sight of the Egyptians, so that they let them have their request. Thus they plundered the Egyptians.
> —Exodus 12:36

This model is an example to this generation. We are living in a day of promise, foreseen and foretold by many saints and prophets throughout the ages. According to the book of Hebrews, innumerable devoted champions saw and longed for this day of prophetic promise . . . and they made spiritual deposits toward its fulfillment. It is our great privilege to be the beneficiaries of a spiritual heritage that transcends our own portion of Church history.

The Lord Jesus has orchestrated history so that every generation of saints can participate in the grand unfolding of His divine plan. Most have already proceeded to Heaven and into the "cloud of witnesses." Their investment of prayer and sacrifice has formed a platform for us. Although they had won divine approval and obtained a testimony of favor from God, they were not permitted to see the fulfillment of the promise in their generation. God planned for something greater by ordaining that they would not come to perfection without us.

> *The Lord Jesus has orchestrated history so that every generation of saints can participate in the grand unfolding of His divine plan.*

Their lives of prayer, sacrifice, and devotion were spiritual seeds of purpose and destiny; we will reap an inheritance as their spiritual heirs. Many in our generation have also sown into this harvest. Loved ones taken prematurely have also invested in the fruitfulness of this day by submitting to the call of God.

### Christ Our Redeemer

Our redemption and destiny were secured solely through the sacrificial offering and resurrection of the Lord Jesus. Without His blood and triumph over death, no plan of redemption or end-time strategy would exist. All who share in eternal life are grafted into His covenant and achieve victory through His blood. There is no other way to the Father; Jesus is the only mediator between God and humanity.

We must fully understand that our redemption and inheritance were purchased by Christ's sacrifice. Yet there is also a Kingdom mystery surrounding the deposit of His Spirit throughout the ages. This mystery connects generations of victorious, overcoming saints in the strategy of Heaven. We, in the Church, are about to receive a stronger understanding of the "cloud of witnesses" and their function. Hebrews 11:39-40 reminds us:

> And all these, having gained approval through their
> faith, did not receive what was promised, because God
> had provided something better for us, so that apart
> from us they would not be made perfect.

The Holy Spirit clearly expressed in this Scripture that "they"—those who sacrificially offered their lives for the cause of Christ—would not be made perfect apart from us. Only in this generation will we see the fullness of this profound mystery fully consummated. The Lord has strategically planned for a latter-day consolidation of the sacrificial lives, prayers, and persecutions of these fervent saints and patriarchs.

A spiritual partnership between the "cloud of witnesses" and the anointed, end-times Body of Christ will be forged. We are privileged to live in the age that will witness the fullness of this promise. The Lord Himself pronounced a blessing on us, saying:

> Blessed are the eyes which see the things you see, for I
> say to you, that many prophets and kings wished to see

the things which you see, and did not see them, and to
hear the things which you hear, and did not hear them.
—Luke 10:23–24

The divine response to all the prayers of the saints, along
with the unfulfilled promises and spiritual sacrifices from
prior generations, will be harnessed and deposited into the
Body of Christ.

It is profound to think that the apostle Paul prayed for you
and me in this generation. He prayed to see the promise of God
fully manifested in the earth. His prayer along with the  prayers
of the saints throughout history were captured as incense in
Heaven and saved for this present generation. Clearly Paul's
writings seem to indicate he did not expect the promise to be so
long in coming. Nonetheless his prayers have been harnessed,
along with those of the many millions of saints since him, for a
divine orchestration of God's purpose.

This cloud of witnesses obtained a testimony from God,
has found favor in God's sight, and now minister from a place
of rest. In some way, they are given heavenly duties and
responsibilities by their Captain, the Lord Himself.

## Obtaining Promises

Great activity exists among the great cloud of witnesses surrounding the end-time Church. These are individuals who,
throughout their lifetime, obtained promises from the Lord.
Through the demonstration of their faith these witnesses won
the right to oversee the stewardship and fulfillment of the
promises they received.

Many saints, even in recent generations, pressed in to the
Lord and received divine pledges of restoration and revival.
Perhaps a praying grandmother spent years before the Lord

until He extended His scepter and rewarded her faithfulness with a promise of revival to her city. By virtue of that distinction, she carries the stewardship of that promise even into eternity. Those who sow and those who reap rejoice together, as the Lord said:

> He who reaps receives wages, and gathers fruit for eternal life, that both he who sows and he who reaps may rejoice together. For in this the saying is true: 'One sows and another reaps.' I sent you to reap that for which you have not labored; others have labored, and you have entered into their labors.
>
> —John 4:36–38, NIV

Every prayer will be answered. Every intercessory tear sown for revival has been captured by the Lord and will be rewarded with a bountiful spiritual harvest. Those who sowed the seeds of revival may not see the fullness in their generation but, still they will rejoice with the individuals privileged to be the beneficiaries of their labor. This generation will enter into the work and promises of prior saints and reap where they have not labored.

*We are living in the day in which the books of Heaven are going to be opened and justice exacted for the many treacherous acts committed against God's people throughout the ages.*

We are living in the day in which the books of Heaven are going to be opened and justice exacted for the many treacherous acts committed against God's people throughout the ages. Deposits of innocent blood are remembered by the Lord. Acknowledgment—and full compensation—will be made for their labor and sacrifice. Every prayer submitted by the righteous of old is preserved in Heaven. An angel will gather that prayerful incense from the altar and release it to the earth in an unprecedented display of grace.

## Unprecedented Grace

The spiritual dynamic of unprecedented grace is not only applicable to those who have lived in years past but also to the sacrifice made by God's people today. Darkness, death, sickness, and demonic strategies have increased as the enemy works to steal the destiny of Heaven from this generation. Recompense and justice for these wrongs will be rendered.

Many families have lost loved ones to sickness, disease, accidents, suicide, and many other tragedies. Even so, not one soul has gone without the Lord's notice. When we come before the Lord and request justice, we can faithfully rest in the knowledge that a spiritual harvest will be exacted. This truth will begin to break the spirit of grief that has paralyzed many within the Body of Christ.

Greater comprehension of the spiritual dimensions in which we are seated will be given in this generation. We function in a dual capacity: we are both natural and spiritual beings. The more spiritually minded we become, the greater our ability to operate in the spiritual domain. God is calling the Body of Christ to a greater maturity in which He will reveal the mysteries of the Kingdom and the economy of Heaven. A revelatory anointing is being granted to the Church to provide insight into God's plan.

## The Prayers of All the Saints

The Bible teaches that there are reservoirs of prayer in Heaven that will be merged with the intercession and sacrifice of the

Lord Jesus Himself. Furthermore, this deposit of prayer will be captured in a censer containing a coal from the altar of the heavenly tabernacle and released back to the earth in an explosive demonstration of the Lord's victory. Loyal and devoted saints of old, as well as loved ones taken prematurely and at the height of their anointing, will witness and share in the fruit of the end-time ministry that is about to unfold.

> Another angel came and stood at the altar, holding a golden censer; and much incense was given to him, so that he might add it to the prayers of all the saints on the golden altar which was before the throne. And the smoke of the incense, with the prayers of the saints, went up before God out of the angel's hand. Then the angel took the censer and filled it with the fire of the altar, and threw it to the earth; . . .
>
> —Revelation 8:3-5

Much has been invested in this day. An overcoming army is being prepared and will be clothed in the garments of Heaven. They will carry significant spiritual authority and power and be privileged to inherit the promises long foreseen throughout the ages. This army will demonstrate the Kingdom of Heaven on earth and taste the good Word of God (Hebrews 6:5).

We are presently at the dawning of a new day in Church history—a glorious history that displays the convergence of the human with the divine. This new day will introduce a much more exhaustive awareness of divine mysteries concerning the end of time.

CHAPTER
9

# THEY OBTAINED PROMISES

ebrews teaches us that a select body of people holds a very distinguished position in Heaven. Those listed in Hebrews 11 are a sample of an assembly who have "obtained a testimony" before God. Their faith and abandoned hearts give them special stature with Christ.

Divine approval rested on them because of their consecrated lives and willingness to yield themselves to the plans and purposes of Heaven. Those listed in Hebrews 11 are simply a sliver of those who have been included in the cloud of witnesses.

They are men and women of incredible faith who saw Heaven's plan and invested themselves in it. Through revelatory vision they beheld God's promise for a righteous generation and longed to see its realization. They made substantial spiritual contributions through prayer, sacrifice, and the administration of the revealed Word.

But the fullness of the promise did not come to fruition in their generation; still they sowed into it. Among God's noble spiritual champions are people who were stoned to death, cut in two, slaughtered by the sword, and burned at the stake. They were men and women willing to suffer hardship by living in caves. Many were openly ridiculed and mocked, cruelly treated, tortured, and wrongly imprisoned. Interestingly, amidst these incredible hardships and oppressions that were imposed on this company of God's friends, we discover that they "obtained promises" (verse 33).

**Stewards of Promise**
It is humbling to read of the individuals who gallantly pressed through excruciating difficulties and hardship to come before God's throne of grace. Through their great faith they:

> conquered kingdoms, performed acts of righteousness, obtained promises, shut the mouths of lions, quenched the power of fire, escaped the edge of the sword, from weakness were made strong, became mighty in war, put foreign armies to flight.
> —Hebrews 11:33–34

The stewards of God's promises won divine approval and achieved their testimonies as His friends. These men and women were biblical and historical giants of faith. To receive a promise of this stature is not as simple as one might think, because to acquire a decisive promise from God carrying far-reaching ramifications requires sacrifice. A massive spiritual price must be paid in order to be granted such privileges. When this promise is realized, these individuals become its stewards in this life and in the life to come.

Abraham was described as a friend of God. He gained divine approval and found favor with God. As a result the Lord pledged that He would bless Abraham and his seed. He promised the patriarch that He would one day visit his children while they suffered in the bondage of Egypt. He swore He would deliver them with His mighty hand and give them an incredible fortune.

Abraham was dead long before the Lord delivered on His promise. Remembering that solemn pledge, God searched for a deliverer to fulfill it. The Bible says:

> For he remembered his holy promise given to his
>     servant Abraham.
> He brought out His people with rejoicing, his chosen
>     ones with shouts of joy.
> —Psalm 105:42–43, NIV

The promise had been made to Abraham, but future generations became beneficiaries of that pledge centuries later. Numerous overcomers throughout the ages have persevered to gain a testimony of favor with God. In the midst of their sufferings and hardship, they were given promises by Heaven according to God's plans. A righteous generation will inherit this heavenly blueprint and bring all its divine promises to fruition.

## Carriers of Heavenly Burdens

I have a friend who was translated to Heaven. He was shown many wonderful things during this encounter, including a scene that gave him great understanding about the role of the cloud of witnesses.

My friend was allowed to observe two men in agonizing

intercession over South Africa. He watched as these men poured their hearts out, weeping over the promise given to them while they lived on the earth. Each was awarded a vow from God that he would see revival come to that nation. Touched, my friend asked one of his angelic escorts who those men were. He was told that one was John G. Lake, and the other was Andrew Murray. At the time he didn't know the history of either man or about their missionary callings in South Africa.

John G. Lake was a man who lived sacrificially for many years in the harvest field of South Africa. He and his family endured great hardships in this spiritual endeavor. Into South Africa's spiritual soil, he sowed his own wife, who died, according to many accounts, of exhaustion and malnutrition. Many of the other leaders and missionaries who labored with Lake and his team also perished; they became spiritual seeds for a promised revival in that nation.

*In the midst of their sacrifice and suffering they obtained the promise to see a visitation of God in that nation.*

Lake yielded his will to the Father and allowed the Holy Spirit to be fully enthroned in his spirit, soul, and body. He gained God's approval and so was promised a revival in South Africa. Even now, among the distinguished company of witnesses in Heaven, he continues to bear a burden for South Africa. He and the others join the intercessory ministry of the Lord Jesus to see the plans of Heaven fulfilled in this day.

Both of these men labored diligently in South Africa and won divine approval for their service to the Lord. In the midst of their sacrifice and suffering they obtained the promise to see a visitation of God in that nation. Someone, someday, will emerge with a loyal, humble, and faithful heart and become the beneficiary of that great commission. As Moses reaped the fruit of the oath given to Abraham, someone will be heir to the deep reservoirs of prayer and suffering invested into revival in South Africa.

### Face-to-Face Encounter with the Lord

Wanda and I have been privileged to have Bob Jones as a close friend for more than ten years. We traveled extensively with Bob for a number of years and have written many of the revelations given to this prophet. We include a number of his revelatory encounters in this book because of their incredible significance and to honor him for the impartation that has come from Heaven to us through him.

Like the saints highlighted in Hebrews 11, Bob has also endured misfortune and difficulty imposed upon him by the adversary. Nevertheless what the enemy intended for evil, God has used for good.

On August 8, 1975, Bob died. Although the enemy desired to end his prophetic ministry in its infancy, the Lord intervened to impart revelation and promise and to bring him back from death.

A number of prophetic revelations involving national and international issues were entrusted to him during the early years. He was releasing them to the corporate body through various church and ministry outlets. Because of the "light" the supernatural insights were bringing, the enemy assigned a spirit of death to stop the prophetic words. The enemy wanted to kill him. Thankfully the Lord used this opportunity to make a divine promise to him in a face-to-face encounter.

### Bob's Death Experience

Bob first began his public prophetic ministry in 1969. As a young boy, he experienced three supernatural encounters while living on a cotton farm in rural Arkansas. The first occurred one August afternoon in 1939 on a dusty road near his home. As he was walking along the hot road, he saw a most unusual sight. He watched as a man riding on a white horse began galloping toward him from Heaven. When he saw that supernatural being, his mind could think of only one thing— a song he had often heard sung in the Baptist churches of Arkansas. He had always been taught that the angel Gabriel would someday appear and blow his trumpet, signifying the end of the world.

Indeed the angelic messenger carried a unique silver trumpet. It had one mouthpiece but two horns, which the angel blew. Even as a young boy, Bob knew this was the angel Gabriel—a recognition that has since been confirmed to him in subsequent experiences. Needless to say, Bob was terrified at the sight. Nothing was spoken. Draped across the saddle of the white horse was a mantle like the hide of an animal. Gabriel tossed the heavenly mantle at Bob's feet and vanished.

Bob has since discovered that this spiritual mantle was worn by a prophet from South Africa who formerly walked the rivers from village to village with a powerful ministry of truth and deliverance. Bob has met the grandson of this man and discussed the ministry the man's grandfather carried to his generation.

**The Messenger**
The angelic messenger seemed to be over six feet tall. He wore a white garment of light that looked like wool. He did not appear to be overly muscular like many warring angels, but his appearance was of noble and weighty stature.

For years the fear resulting from that experience of his boyhood caused Bob to run from the ultimate commission and mandate placed on his life. Even though he was not faithfully serving the Lord during his early adult years, a deep sense of conviction filled him.

It wasn't until September 1969 that he began to function in the prophetic ministry ordained for him. At that time he agreed with the Lord to wear the prophet's mantle brought to him as a young boy. Immediately after accepting his call, Bob began to view scenes in the spirit that were very difficult for his natural mind to fathom. The Holy Spirit allowed him to see, and hear, images of young babies weeping as their lives were being ended prematurely. Prophetically he was seeing the onslaught of abortion.

> *The Holy Spirit allowed him to see, and hear, images of young babies weeping as their lives were being ended prematurely. Prophetically he was seeing the onslaught of abortion.*

During the early 1970s these visionary encounters continued and showed the emergence of rampant homosexuality and abortion. As Bob shared these visions publicly, his listeners struggled with the prophecies. Many leaders and fellowships could not accept the revelation of such spiritual malaise becoming prevalent in our country.

## A Demonic Threat

On August 7, 1975, Bob Jones was given an incredible vision that illustrated the escalation of homosexuality and a deadly disease that would be communicated from it. The vision also illustrated how abortion would proliferate to such a degree that science would eventually develop a pill a woman could swallow to abort a child. These revelations were quite profound for the mid-'70s.

On August 8, the day after this horrific insight, an evil spirit appeared to Bob. The demon threatened to release the spirit of death against Bob if he shared publicly these future satanic plans the Lord had showed him. Initially Bob did not believe this wicked messenger had the authority to take his life, so he immediately prophesied what he had seen. Surprisingly the evil spirit made good on his promise—somehow touching Bob's body, causing what the doctors believed was an arterial rupture.

Bob began to bleed profusely from his mouth and nose. The lower part of his body hardened as it filled with fluid. He was in unbearable pain. The medical prognosis was not good; the doctors prescribed analgesic medication to help relieve the agonizing pain and suffering. Bob lay on a bed and covered his face with a towel to help capture the flow of blood pouring from his mouth.

*At first Bob thought the medication had kicked in. But it wasn't science that eased his strain. Bob Jones had died, passing from this temporal life into the eternal realm.*

Then suddenly the pain lifted. At first Bob thought the medication had kicked in. But it wasn't science that eased his strain. Bob Jones had died, passing from this temporal life into the eternal realm.

## A Visit to Heaven

Bob found himself in a tunnel of light with an angel of the Lord at his right. He looked at his clothes and discovered that he was wearing a sparkling clean white robe. It was then he realized the evil spirit had taken his life. Immediately he felt joy and relief at the purity of his heavenly garments.

The gladness shifted to a brief moment of grief as he was allowed to watch other people who had perished at precisely the same moment. Unfortunately they were not shrouded in garments of light. Instead he watched ninety-seven percent of the people who had died descending into the bowels of hell. Each was somehow clothed in accoutrements of what had been his or her god on earth. Bob was devastated at the sight.

**The Door of Heaven**

Three people traveled with Bob as they ascended toward a great Light embodying Heaven's door. He was fourth in line and watched as each of them proceeded toward the Light above them. The prominent Light they saw was the Lord Jesus Himself greeting the new arrivals.

First in line was an eleven-year-old girl who was filled with the love of God. Her lot in life had been to lie on a sickbed suffering from a terminal disease. However, she used that time to express the love of Heaven through prayer and intercession for others. She entered the gates of glory with a great reward.

"Did you learn to love?" the Lord asked her.

"Yes!" she answered, beaming as she entered into His abundant blessings.

Next in line was a large African American woman, surrounded by a large number of angels. Bob asked the angel of the Lord standing to his right why she had so many ministering spirits with her. He was told she had been a powerful evangelist on the earth; the angels assigned to her labored together with her in ministry. As this woman prayed and interceded for the salvation of others, the ministering spirits would be commissioned to go to those for whom she was praying. Released through her prayers, they were empowered with the authority of Heaven to bring those individuals into the Kingdom. Great was her reward also.

"Did you learn to love?" the Lord asked her.

"Yes!" she replied, and passed into His heart.

Standing directly in front of Bob was a ninety-three-year-old woman who appeared to have been crippled by arthritis. The hardships and failures of her life, seemed to have embittered her. While she maintained her love for God, she was unable to express that same love to others. A root of bitterness had defiled her soul. Though she entered Heaven as her eternal home, she carried no fruit or victorious testimony as her reward. When the Lord asked her, "Did you learn to love?" she responded that she loved Him but had not learned to love others. In that setting, it was impossible to lie; the only answer she could give was the truth. Therefore she entered but had no fruit to present to Him.

### A Divine Pledge

Bob was next to join the Lord's heart and enter the gates of Heaven—or so he thought! Pointing His finger at Bob, the Lord proclaimed, "You must return." Bob was stunned that he was not allowed to enter as those before him had done.

"You have not completed your course, and the enemy has violated the destiny of Heaven created for you," Christ told him.

Satan had intruded upon Bob's life by prematurely killing him. The imposition of the adversary was not because of some rebellion or act of disobedience on Bob's part but was instead an unjust act attempting to abort the plan and strategy of Heaven. It was a vile attempt to silence a prophetic voice that would help prepare a righteous generation to demonstrate the Kingdom of Heaven on earth. Because of this violation, the Lord, according to His system of justice, was able to impart a great blessing. What the enemy had intended for evil, God was going to use for a noble cause.

As was the case with the overcomers recorded in Hebrews 11, the enemy's attack had allowed God to deliver a promise to earth. In this face-to-face encounter—caused by the enemy's hand—Bob was given a pledge by Jesus Himself. The Lord promised to demonstrate, in unprecedented ways, the virtue of Heaven in a generation soon to arise.

"You must return to the earth to touch a few of My leaders and prepare them for the harvest I am going to bring in the last days," Jesus told him. "I am going to glorify Myself beyond anything that has happened previously in the world. I am going to bring one billion souls to Myself, and this plan of Heaven will begin in the year 2000."

> *"I am going to glorify Myself beyond anything that has happened previously in the world. I am going to bring one billion souls to Myself, and this plan of Heaven will begin in the year 2000."*

The Lord specifically promised that end-time purposes would be launched and accelerated at this strategic time, which would mark the beginning of a call to maturity in the Body of Christ.

The Lord told Bob that by the year 2000, millions of people would be dying from the disease about which he had been prophesying. The Lord also instructed him that those numbers would exponentially escalate until there was sweeping repentance from sin.

## Returning to the Earth

For the promise of spiritual awakening and the harvest of souls, Bob was willing to return to the earth and continue the prophetic ministry entrusted to him. The Lord informed Bob that before his death he would see God's glory coming to the earth in a massive harvest of souls.

God told Bob that the incredible miracles, signs, and wonders that we read in Scripture are only a tithe of what is coming. Every supernatural ministry, prophetic gift, and heavenly endowment we discover in the Bible will function in an amplified way during the coming days.

Bob had obtained a promise from the Lord. Almighty God will faithfully see that promise fulfilled—He cannot lie. Today, many people like Bob are pressing through various difficulties and are obtaining promises for revival, restoration, and revelation of Heaven's glory.

## Resurrection Angels

An interesting validation was given to Bob's death experience. As Bob was brought back into his room, he observed his body lying on the bed, covered by a bloody towel. The spirit of death was standing in the corner of the room. However, two angels were beside his bed. These were "resurrection angels." In Scripture we read of two angels at the tomb of our Lord at the time of His resurrection. When the Lord Jesus chooses to bring someone back from death, He dispatches ministering spirits who carry resurrection power.

Bob was allowed to listen as the two angels conversed with each other about future events. One angel announced there would be a gathering of fifty thousand Christians in the Harry Truman Sports Complex. The other angel responded that an even larger gathering of saints would take place in Washington, D.C. He affirmed that the number gathered in Kansas City would only be a tithe of those converging on Washington.

The angels specifically mentioned that the first meeting

would be held in the Truman Sports Complex to honor that former president for the position he took in establishing Israel as a recognized nation. That act captured the attention of Heaven and pleased the Lord. Although President Truman may have made many mistakes, this one item was of monumental importance. Because of Truman's willingness to stand with Israel, God honored his name and caused a strategic meeting to happen at that specific location.

After regaining his strength, Bob shared publicly the following Sunday what he had heard during his death experience. He prophesied about the meeting that would take place in Kansas City and the subsequent one in Washington, D. C. Two years later, in 1977, the initial gathering took place, fulfilling the prophecy and validating the revelations gained in Bob's death experience. The North American Renewal Service Committee (NARSC) assembly that met, fifty-thousand strong, in the Truman Sports Complex in July 1977 was the fulfillment of the first prophecy.

The greater meeting took place in the 1980 Washington for Jesus rally, where approximately five hundred thousand people gathered to pray for a national revival and spiritual awakening.

Our Father has a purpose, design, and destiny for our lives and well-being. It is only by abiding in the Vine that we will sustain fruitfulness. There is much more to the unveiling of the divine Kingdom than simply embracing a heavenly domain, although that is rewarding beyond comprehension. God is calling a people who qualify as His sons and daughters and who will reign with Him in a company of overcomers.

PART
# III

# BIRTHING
# HEAVENLY
# PURPOSES

# THE PRINCE of PERSIA

**D**aniel was a prophet who was highly regarded in Heaven. Rarely do we find such affectionate salutations from God as those He expressed to Daniel. Much of Daniel's revelation and many of his visionary encounters centered on a future generation identified as the "latter days" (literally "end of the days). He was a forerunner of a company of end-time saints who will be esteemed by God and awarded mighty revelatory inspiration and insight. In many ways God's role in Daniel's life offers a prophetic model for us to follow.

Likewise, we can also use Daniel's model to discern the enemy's plans against the destinies of God's people. In Daniel 10, for example, we read of one of the incredible visitations bestowed on this important prophet. However, that prophetic experience was not without intense resistance from unseen sinister forces.

In his vision Daniel discovered a dark entity called the

prince of Persia. This principality is once again trying to stop the hand of Heaven from reaching God's covenant people. Like Daniel, much of the Church has been in a posture of repentance and prayer, seeking the favor of God.

Daniel 10 is a fascinating portion of Scripture highlighting a present confrontation and spiritual opportunity. It recounts such awesome attributes of the heavenly realm that even a righteous servant such as Daniel was overwhelmed. It vividly details the spiritual conflict taking place and the vital role we play in it. When we come humbly before God, He imparts essential strategies and insight to us.

Daniel 10 followed the decree which had been issued by Cyrus allowing the Jewish people to return to their homeland. Even so, only a remnant had responded, and they faced much difficulty and hardship.

Most of the Jewish community remained woven into Babylonian society and ignored this fulfillment of Jeremiah's prophecies. Heartbroken, Daniel carried Heaven's burden with mourning and personal sacrifice, setting the stage for his tremendous encounter with the heavenly realm.

> *The revivals of the twentieth century pointed people to Christ and out of the cold, formal religion that denied His power.*

In many ways a similar call of return to our heritage and homeland came during the previous generation. The revivals of the twentieth century pointed people to Christ and out of the cold, formal religion that denied His power. This struggle was not without intense conflict and defiance; nevertheless, it has forged a body of people who know the rich heritage established by the early apostolic Church and promised to the latter-day Body of Christ. They know their God and will do mighty exploits for His glory.

## Prophetic Strategy

In January 1999 Wanda and I took part in a gathering of leaders seeking insight from the Lord for the coming seasons. Historically these strategy sessions consisted of fifteen to twenty men and women joining together to pursue the Lord through prayer and the use of revelatory gifts in an informal setting. Each person would relate his or her piece of the strategic puzzle in hope of developing a more complete picture of the Lord's blueprint. Throughout the years these meetings have been very fruitful in outlining the Lord's heart for a given season and also identifying plans of the enemy set against the Church and our nation.

In this particular year the Lord delineated specific issues having direct application to the current events at that time in our nation and around the world. In the meetings the Holy Spirit admonished us saying, "Terrorism is not coming . . . it is already here, and an attack is imminent."

The prophecy stated that the attack would come through the unholy alliance of a "religious" and a "political" spirit. This alliance would produce a doubly evil anointing, which would deceptively twist the minds of religious zealots into thinking they were doing good and serving God by acts of violence that would promote evil.

When I first shared these insights during a meeting in Albany, Oregon, a confirmation of this truth was provided the next day through *Newsweek* magazine. Its headline read, ISLAM—THE MERGER OF RELIGION AND STATE. The article went on to outline the Islamic agenda and their radical plans for its fulfillment. (*Note: We must continually remind ourselves that we are strictly against the evil spirit sponsoring Islam, not the people deceived by its doctrine. We believe and pray for a great harvest among the Muslims; perhaps we are on the threshold of seeing that day.*)

### The Birthing of God's Purposes

The Holy Spirit had conveyed to us the enemy's plans and the ultimate purpose of Satan's agenda. In these revelations the Lord specifically told me that the ultimate purpose of the unholy alliance was to "frustrate the birthing of God's purposes in our nation."

The fact that terrorism has struck a devastating blow and continues to be a threat is proof that great end-time objectives are being birthed. Significant power and authority are coming to those groomed and prepared for this day. A company of believers will soon "cross over" to taste the Word of God and the power of the age to come; they will return and share it with the body-at-large, introducing a new day in the Spirit.

The prophetic model we discover in Daniel points to some of the underlying meaning and provides essential understanding of God's plans for this strategic hour. The bride is poised to leave Babylonian captivity and enter her promised liberty and restoration. Leadership, in the pattern of Daniel, Joshua, and Zerubbabel, is emerging to steer the Church into rebuilding its lost heritage and recovering its promised inheritance. The Lord is sending revelatory insight and heavenly provision for this purpose while the adversary is once again stirring the prince of Persia in an effort to withstand the mandates of God.

The warring hosts of Heaven are being dispatched and energized through intercessory prayer to overcome the enemy's resistance so that the visitation can be realized. That is why there is such a need for spiritual focus. Satan's strategy is to distract and divide in his attempt to stop, or at least postpone, the order of end-time confrontations. He is trying to promote conflicts and induce ordained spiritual engagements before their proper time and the complete preparation of the bride of Christ. The

Church's role, in accord with God's plan, is to counter the enemy's plan with prayer, praise, and prophetic proclamation.

### The Lord's Holy Alliance

In the 1999 leader's meeting, the Lord emphasized that His "holy alliance" was the antidote for the enemy's devices. God intends to endow a generation of overcomers with the spirit of revelation and position them, in power and authority, as watchers on the walls of the Church. These people will facilitate a holy partnership of revelatory anointing and intercessory prayer with true spiritual authority. They will provide continual prayer, anointed worship, and prophetic declaration.

Daniel's prophetic portrait is a helpful paradigm of Heaven's strategy in this confrontation. Daniel focused his attention on Heaven, through prayer and fasting, in order to understand the spiritual conflict raging in the spiritual realm. He received a visitation from Heaven in response to his devotion. The divine attributes we read about in this passage also provide foresight into the Lord's revelation about the struggle we presently face. The Lord admonished us in 1999: "This is not to be touched by human hands, that is, human perceptions, traditions, and formulas. Instead, what is being birthed will be Spirit-led and Spirit-sponsored."

Everything manifested in radical Islamic strongholds is directed in the heavenlies against the purposes the Lord desires to release to us. However, as the Scriptures point out:

From the days of John the Baptist until now the kingdom of heaven suffers violence, and the violent take it by force.
—Matthew 11:12, NKJV

If we truly hunger to see God's spiritual government

birthed and functioning, we must take our post and gain the Lord's authority through prayer and declaring our agreement with Heaven. That is the divine strategy for this season.

### The Coming Government

Daniel humbled himself before the Lord and petitioned God for wisdom for His covenant people. The Bible records that Daniel's answer was promptly released from the throne but was delayed for twenty-one days by the prince of Persia. In similar fashion many of God's people have humbled themselves and prayed the Daniel 9 prayer of repentance and awakening. The Lord is releasing the provision desperately needed for their birth. But, once again, the prince of Persia is attempting to postpone Heaven's answer.

Global terrorism, unrest in the Middle East, and war with Iraq are just a few ways this principality seeks to distract, prohibit, and frustrate the birthing of heavenly aspirations in the earth. As in the days of Daniel, we must depend upon God's grace to release warring spirits, commissioned by the Holy Spirit and energized through the saint's prayers, to pave the way for this provision. When we position ourselves contritely with fasting and intercession, we help bring God's promise to fruition.

In 1999 Bob Jones and I prophesied about a building serving as a memorial to humanity and its exploits and accomplishments. We both had separate visions and revelatory words concerning this same issue and the expression of the Lord's heart. At the time neither of us had any idea of the full implications of our revelations or their relationship to cataclysmic events in 2001. The divine communications established a timeline in the Spirit for "latter-day" events.

In Bob's vision he was taken to the pinnacle of a great building representing human prosperity and self-sufficiency.

Much like the tower of Babel, it usurped a place in the hearts of men and women that rightfully belonged to God.

The Holy Spirit apprehended Bob and lifted him above the building in a manner reminiscent of the way Ezekiel was taken into the spirit to see Earth from Heaven's perspective. The Holy Spirit wanted Bob to see, from His point of view, the activities and spiritual influences at the heart of this great building.

Bob was not actually atop the building but elevated above it in the vision. His attention was drawn first to a prominent statue mounted as a memorial on the crown of the building. The monument had the attributes and appearance of an ancient god and represented idolatry.

*At that moment a burst of fire, like lightning, descended against the statue with such intense heat that it cracked and broke into several pieces.*

At that moment a burst of fire, like lightning, descended against the statue with such intense heat that it cracked and broke into several pieces. After the fire a great wind blew against what remained of the monument. The wind blew steadily against the statue with enough velocity to erode what the fire did not burn. After the wind an earthquake struck with such violent trembling that the remaining portion of the memorial fell from the building and crashed to the ground.

The structure had been a tribute to the accomplishments and prosperity of human strength—the foolish pride of humanity acknowledging its own exploits by creating an image in its own glory. The memorial portrayed the very essence of idolatry and the deceptive worship of false gods. It illustrated the insidiousness of self-sufficiency and stiff-necked arrogance.

**Days of Restoration**

The Holy Spirit then lowered Bob to the base of the platform that had previously held the memorial in place. He was given a "great tool" to extract the nuts and bolts securing the base so that even the foundation of this statute was disassembled. What would have been a very difficult task was made simple by using the implement provided by the Holy Spirit.

Fulfilling the mandates and commissions of the latter-day move of God will require impartation of exceptional spiritual gifts. The wisdom and strength afforded through natural abilities simply will not suffice. The seven-fold Spirit of God must rest upon the end-time army and herald the message and ministry of the Kingdom. This is the only weapon that will victoriously overcome the evil spirit that has so deeply entrenched itself in the heart of this nation.

> *Fulfilling the mandates and commissions of the latter-day move of God will require impartation of exceptional spiritual gifts.*

Bob's vision then shifted into a new day. His attention was directed to a spiritual transport carrying an image to replace the destroyed idol. This commemorative representation was a great and glorious one, similar to the famous Iwo Jima Memorial of the American flag being erected on Iwo Jima island. Instead of an American flag, however, the image was a cross being lifted by twelve men. Each man shielded his own face so as not to receive any recognition or glory for the Lord's sacrifice.

The Holy Spirit told Bob to use the same tool he had used to dismantle the previous memorial's foundation to securely and permanently lock the cross in  place. The same spiritual tools used to expose the realm of darkness will also facilitate the full unveiling of the Cross and the Kingdom of Heaven.

The Spirit of the Lord will rest upon emerging leaders in a Luke 4:18 commissioning. A spirit of wisdom and revelation, counsel and might, and knowledge and fear of the Lord will characterize the Kingdom army.

Bob's visionary encounter offers us a valuable spiritual lesson. Often we have wanted to exercise spiritual authority to tear down strongholds and dominions of the adversary. Clearly a portion of our mandate in God's army is to use Christ's authority to overcome the realm of darkness.

Even so, that responsibility must be accompanied by faithfulness to the commission to birth God's Kingdom in place of Satan's. We carry a dual burden to both uproot and plant. The true spiritual government that emerges will supplant evil spiritual influences with the Kingdom's manifestation.

The prophet Jeremiah was commissioned by the Spirit of God to do two things—to tear down and to build up. The enemy's high places must be eradicated but only when we wield the authority to establish in their place genuine spiritual communities that occupy the ground taken in those confrontations. As the Lord told Jeremiah,

> See, I have appointed you this day over the nations
> and over the kingdoms,
> To pluck up and to break down,
> To destroy and to overthrow,
> To build and to plant.
> —Jeremiah 1:10

The twelve self-effacing soldiers represented the coming government of God that will raise the cross above all else. This government will introduce the glorious reality and power of redemption purchased through the blood of Jesus to the Body of Christ. The mantle of authority it brings will include the dual tasks of dismantling and planting.

When the Israelites entered the Promised Land, it was crucially important for them to occupy the land as it was being secured. Otherwise, while they were distracted by contending in other conflicts, the enemy would reinfiltrate the area with enhanced strength. It is the Lord's design not only to expose realms of darkness but also to convey light.

God is about to reveal through His governmental design an authority to teach and preach about the cross in a profound and powerful way. The Body of Christ has scarcely touched the great redemptive truths of the cross; these will prepare the bride for her union with the Bridegroom. As in all wars, liberty and freedom come with a price. These realities will be imparted to those willing to consider the cost and pay it freely. We pay the price by allowing the pruning of the Holy Spirit so we may know Christ, the power of His resurrection, and the fellowship of His sufferings.

## Establishing the Foundation

The primary responsibility of apostles, prophets, evangelists, pastors, and teachers will be to securely fashion the foundation of the cross to people's hearts. As in all genuine expressions of revival, the demonstration of the Spirit and His power is a prerequisite. Heavenly mandates can only be achieved through the tools provided by the Holy Spirit.

A desperate and lovesick people, embodying the heart of David and his reckless abandonment for God, will develop. They will be a "one thing" company with a single-minded desire to experience an intimate relationship with Jesus. They will be identified as the friends of God, and they will have but one agenda—to dwell in the house of the Lord all the days of their lives and gaze upon His beauty.

Retreat or slowdown are not options. As we accelerate toward the Lord ignoring all obstacles, He will in His abundant grace see us through and position us on His highway of holiness.

In 1999 Bob and I had no inkling that the vision of the memorial could be interpreted as the spiritual targets of the religious zealots on September 11. As we view those events in retrospect and apply them to the prophetic word, we can now directly see that the vision's signposts indicate where we are prophetically standing at this moment in history.

The third wave of destruction in Bob's vision was an earthquake that overcame the memorial. News reports documented that the collapse of the twin towers comprising the World Trade Center on September 11, 2001, registered on the Richter scale. Like many prophetic events presented in Scripture, this is a signpost to believers to identify our place in history and the provision God has established for us. We must be awakened to this day of destiny.

Biblically twelve is the number of governmental and apostolic design. The twelve humble soldiers erecting the cross represented the apostolic governmental reformation presently in motion. The Lord, through the prophet Joel, promised that He would restore all that has been devoured by the adversary. Our apostolic heritage has been undermined by an Antichrist spirit.

> *The Lord, through the prophet Joel, promised that He would restore all that has been devoured by the adversary.*

Even so, since the days of Martin Luther, we have experienced a progressive restoration of our heritage. We are now on the threshold of witnessing the unveiling of apostolic leaders in the order of the early Church. From there we can move even deeper into the rich heritage foretold for the latter days.

Following the tragedy of September 11, news agencies circulated photographs of the debris remaining at Ground Zero. One photo evidenced a huge iron crossbeam that had come to rest atop a mountain of twisted metal and Sheetrock. This metal cross seemed to constitute further affirmation of the vision's prophetic significance and present application. I believe this symbol was divinely constructed to nurture hope and faith in the midst of tragedy.

The brutal destruction of Jerusalem in A.D. 70 was a tragic event, yet the Holy Spirit used this fulfillment of prophecy to disperse the disciples and catalyze the preaching of the Gospel to every tribe, tongue, people, and nation throughout the known world of that day. The Holocaust, in which six million Jews perished during World War II, was the greatest immolation of our time; yet out of the ashes of concentration camp gas chambers the Lord birthed the State of Israel. New days are birthed out of severe hardship and tragedy.

### Eyes Opened to the True Battlefield

The confrontation between light and darkness is presently escalating in the spirit realm. Our role in the conflict is to call upon the Lord to release the spiritual resources and trained heavenly warriors to meet the challenge of this engagement. Centuries ago, the prophet Elisha and his servant beheld a vivid illustration of this spiritual reality.

As an invading army surrounded his home, Elisha stood with faith and assurance while his servant stood shocked by Elisha's conviction until his spiritual eyes were opened to perceive its source. The prophet did not fear what his natural eyes could observe, because he relied on the spiritual awareness gained by revelatory insight. When the servant looked again at the scene once the scales had been removed from his spiritual eyes, he saw that the real battle would be won in the spirit realm where the supernatural armies of Heaven far outnumbered the natural armies of the opposing king.

> Now when the attendant of the man of God had risen early and gone out, behold, an army with horses and chariots was circling the city. And his servant said to him, "Alas, my master! What shall we do?" So he answered, "Do not fear, for those who are with us are more than those who are with them." Then Elisha prayed and said, "O LORD, I pray, open his eyes that he may see." And the LORD opened the servant's eyes and he saw; and behold, the mountain was full of horses and chariots of fire all around Elisha.
>
> —2 Kings 6:15–17

Spiritual vision replaces fear with faith and fainting with the courage derived from an understanding that there are more with us than with the enemy. Nothing changed in this scenario except Elisha's servant's perception. Without question his faith level soared, for suddenly, his expectation was not solely based on what his natural eyes could discern. His spiritual vision showed him the full panoply of Heaven's armies and the tableau of the true battle's course.

When God's people bombard Heaven with prayer and intercession for the release of the Lord of Hosts and His troops, they are spiritually fortified. Angelic warriors and fiery chariots arrive to equip and support God's covenant soldiers.

The struggle is won or lost on the unseen battlefield through prayer, intercession, and prophetic proclamations. We must agree with Heaven to empower the Kingdom of Light to overcome and have dominion over the domain of darkness.

While we cannot ignore the natural arena, our focus must be trained in the same plane Elisha accessed through eyes that perceive the revelatory realm of Heaven.

### The Heavenly Places

On five separate occasions in his letter to the Ephesians, Paul highlights "heavenly places" as the seat of dominion for activities taking place on earth. Our blessings are located in heavenly places along with the principalities and powers set against our inheritance. Therein lies the conflict.

The heavenly places are a spiritual domain coexistent with the natural realm. In the spirit are strongholds and dominions, along with spiritual beings equipped with swords, battle armament, and other spiritual weaponry. The heavenly places are not some far distant land but a celestial realm surrounding us. As Paul describes it:

> The righteousness of faith speaks in this way, "Do not say in your heart, 'Who will ascend into heaven?' (that is, to bring Christ down from above) or, 'Who will descend into the abyss?' (that is, to bring Christ up from the dead). But what does it say? 'The word is near you, in your mouth and in your heart' (that is, the word of faith which we preach)."
> —Romans 10:6–8, NKJV

The heavenly places contain the blessings and incorruptible inheritance we need to fulfill our mandate. However, we must contend for them by means of revelatory insight and mobilized faith. Our true citizenship and biblical bill of rights are from Heaven. Because of the Lord's overcoming victory, He has been raised above all principalities and powers. The supremacy He regained for us is now being delegated to us but must be appropriated by those who believe in His victory.

In Daniel 10 the prince of Persia tried to withstand the heavenly messenger's visitation. In like fashion the devil's army is deploying diabolical schemes to oppose the divine strategies and purposes in the Book of Destiny. It is the same spiritual hindrance that confronted Daniel.

Satan is aware of the present hour of destiny, and his general, the prince of Persia, is once again attempting to withstand this heavenly release by launching spiritual influences against the divine destinies of God's people.

The prince of Persia was a prevailing evil principality who apparently possessed an ability to oppose, or at least hinder, the delivery of spiritual messages. This satanic agent was associated with the Persian kingdom and vigorously opposed Daniel and the birthing of a new day in Israel's history.

*The primary demonic strategy underlying the onslaught of terrorism and political unrest in the Middle East is to frustrate the birth of Kingdom realities in this generation.*

The enemy's plan once again is to divert our focus from doing what is needed to birth God's end-time purposes and government. The primary demonic strategy underlying the onslaught of terrorism and political unrest in the Middle East is to frustrate the birth of Kingdom realities in this generation.

The enemy is well aware of the similarities between the way God delivered His people from Babylonian oppression and today's heavenly mandate to deliver this generation from spiritual confusion! The angel of the Lord who visited Daniel showed him the destinies of nations and insight from the

"Scripture of Truth," also known as the Book of Destiny. He illuminated Daniel as follows:

> Do you know why I have come to you? And now I must return to fight with the prince of Persia; and when I have gone forth, indeed the prince of Greece will come. But I will tell you what is noted in the Scripture of Truth. (No one upholds me against these, except Michael your prince . . . )
>
> —Daniel 10:20–21, NKJV

The Holy Spirit gave Daniel insight into the end-time confrontation between light and darkness. Daniel was also assured that those of God's covenant people who have understanding will shine brilliantly and do great exploits for the Kingdom sake. Many of the truths Daniel was shown were sealed and hidden in God's heart until the last days.

We are invited into the heavenly arena to apprehend the secrets and mysteries hidden in the mind of Christ. Jesus' heart is a great treasury of wisdom, knowledge, mystery, and hidden manna. The god of this world has orchestrated an all-out assault to stop, or at least delay, the acquisition of these essential gifts.

## Supernatural Endowments

In many ways Daniel and his three friends represent how the Lord will equip His army for special assignments. The Babylonian captivity of the Jewish people provides a prophetic portrait of the Body of Christ's condition and a hint of the Lord's promise of spiritual deliverance.

Daniel 1:17 describes the special empowerment from Heaven imparted to the former. God gave them knowledge and "intelligence in every branch of literature and wisdom;

Daniel even understood all kinds of visions and dreams."

The Lord gave them revelatory knowledge and intelligence in various matters of writing and literature. Bestowing by spiritual transference the blessing of unique knowledge and exceptional capacity in literature and all manner of written work. The Lord quickened in them special skills to apprehend and articulate spiritual understanding and heavenly wisdom. Daniel was notably gifted with supernatural perception into all manner of visions and dreams. God had empowered them to excel in governmental scholarship.

This pattern will also apply in this day when the Lord discovers the devoted obedient hearts of the spiritually strong. Then vast storehouses of revelatory insight and supernatural knowledge concerning Scripture, creation, science, the arts, and many other subjects will be entrusted to believers who follow the model of Daniel and his three friends. These four young men provide a prophetic standard of those who know their God intimately and accomplish great exploits. These friends of God will engage the revelatory realm of Heaven. They will be marked by their excellent spirit and granted acute perception and understanding to interpret dreams and visions, clarify revelatory experiences, and solve difficult and enigmatic problems. They will be people who receive insight from the throne room and respond to God's invitation to be shown future secrets.

*Then vast storehouses of revelatory insight and supernatural knowledge concerning Scripture, creation, science, the arts, and many other subjects will be entrusted to believers who follow the model of Daniel and his three friends.*

During a prophetic experience I had a few years ago the

Lord told me that Daniel 1:17 was spiritually linked to Ephesians 1:17. These are parallel passages offering the same promise with different time frames. One is from the old covenant and outlines God's dealings with humanity during difficult times, pointing to a future day of supernatural intervention in the world. The other, expressed in the new covenant, records the heritage of believers.

Despite our perceived personal limitations or lack of educational opportunities, the Lord is a quickening Spirit. As our legacy, He has promised to impart life to our mortal bodies and to grant us the spirit of revelation to access mysteries, secrets, and revelatory knowledge.

In Roland Buck's throne room experience, two thousand Scriptures and references were immediately imprinted on his mind. Buck reported that the Scriptures were written on his heart and mind in a split second as a printing press inscribes information on paper. Numerous other testimonies exist of individuals who were supernaturally granted the ability to recall the entire Bible from memory.

*Buck reported that the Scriptures were written on his heart and mind in a split second as a printing press inscribes information on paper.*

Many who attended Maria Woodworth-Etter's meetings were caught up in the Spirit to experience visions and revelations from the Lord. In these supernatural encounters with God, some would be commissioned as missionaries to foreign lands; they would emerge from their vision capable of fluently speaking the language of the nation to which they were called.

The Father enjoys revealing His Kingdom to us and performing awesome deeds only He can accomplish. It was a small thing for Him to rejuvenate the bodies of Abraham and

Sarah and quicken them with strength. Even after Sarah's death, Abraham, well over a century old, continued in the strength imparted to him and bore many more sons by Keturah (Genesis 25:1). The Lord is more than able to equip us with the supernatural gifts needed to access the unfathomable treasures hidden in Him.

As the Bible also promises, the Holy Spirit knows what is hidden in darkness and exposes deep and secret things. Light dwells with Him, bringing illumination to what has been set apart and reserved for the generation of destiny (Daniel 2:22).

God promised He would give us the treasures of darkness and the concealed riches of heavenly places so we would know it is the Lord who calls us by our name (Isaiah 45:3). This divine promise supplies both the riches of revelatory insight as well as the natural provisions essential to fulfill the mandate of this *kairos* moment.

Even now, individuals are engaging the revelatory realm of Heaven and receiving downloads of insight into physics, light, sound, and spiritual colors. The apostle John's visit to Heaven's throne room outlined awesome sights, sounds, and vibrant colors surrounding God's seat of dominion and victory. The more understanding we have of that realm, the greater our ability to cooperate with Heaven in demonstrating the Kingdom on earth.

Those being awakened to this realm and seeking understanding in science, physics, and the elements of creation are not super-geniuses with great scientific minds. Most are ordinary Christians who are tapping into God's heart as He releases His mind to the bride. Much will be spoken and written in the coming days involving this dimension of our heritage. As with Einstein, an insatiable desire to understand creation and the Creator will flourish in the hearts of many Christians. Access to the spiritual books of Heaven will be granted in order to provide divine wisdom, revelatory knowledge, and supernatural strategy.

## Books of Strategy

On another occasion in early 2003 I was granted the privilege of seeing a library room of Heaven. This experience began in a similar fashion as Peter's experience on the rooftop in Acts 10:10. It was as if I were in the natural realm one moment and transported into the spiritual the next. I was suddenly standing in an open field. I looked to my right and saw the Lord dressed in a royal blue robe with a sternly focused determination in His countenance. I gingerly walked toward Him and felt compelled to embrace Him, which I did. Ten thousand years would not be enough to stand in that embrace. It was the very embodiment of perfect peace and security. I would have been satisfied to remain there forever.

After a few moments the Lord lifted His right arm and pointed to the object of His focus. I noticed a very securely built stone wall. However, upon closer examination of the specific spot at which the Lord was pointing, I noticed a very small opening I intuitively knew I had to explore.

I approached the wall and the very small opening the Lord had pinpointed, and I discovered that the stone blocks could be maneuvered and displaced. Gradually I removed enough rock to create a hole large enough for me to climb through. When I did, I found myself in an ancient room with many shelves of parchments and books. I intuitively knew these were books of strategy for the generations.

Each book or scroll I saw was written on a material similar to leather. These items were significantly different from the ones in the "treasury room" which appeared to be made from some form of wood. It would have been wonderful to remain in that room for a long period of time to examine the many strategies of God. However, my attention was drawn to a parchment nailed to a wooden post stationed in the center of the room.

The parchment looked like a piece of leather, about six inches long and three inches wide. Three Scriptures were inscribed on it. I am not certain if the Scripture references were printed with some form of ink or burned into the parchment. I removed it from the post and carefully surveyed the three biblical passages identified on it: Psalm 68, Jude, 1 Kings 3.

I immediately knew that each passage specifically related to the calling of the bride in our generation and provided strategy for the release of Heaven and the fulfillment of our bridal mandate.

Psalm 68 is prophetically descriptive of the bridal calling. She will be like the wings of a dove covered with silver and its pinions with glistening gold (verse 13). This portrays the manifest presence of Christ in the revelation of His Kingdom.

Jude identifies the spirit of compromise that will attempt to rob the bride of her inheritance and source of spiritual strength. There are two opposing spirits that will be clearly differentiated in the coming days; no longer will the two be indistinguishable.

1 Kings 3 recounts God's supernatural impartation of wisdom and knowledge into Solomon's life. God has now come to release to us the same spirit of wisdom and revelation that empowered this famous king of Israel. We will not be able to accommodate our mandates fully without these spiritual endowments.

### Eating the Open Scroll

In Revelation 10 we read that John, here representing the bride of Christ, was directed to take an open book from the hand of an angel. John was directed to eat the "opened" book of redemption containing the mysteries of the Kingdom and the full revelation of the Lord Jesus. He was to taste the good word of God and the fullness of the book of redemption.

> Then the voice which I heard from heaven, I heard again speaking with me, and saying, "Go, take the book which is open in the hand of the angel who stands on the sea and on the land."
>
> So I went to the angel, telling him to give me the little book. And he said to me, "Take it and eat it; it will make your stomach bitter, but in your mouth it will be sweet as honey . . ."
>
> And they said to me, "You must prophesy again concerning many peoples and nations and tongues and kings."
> —Revelation 10:8–11

When something is eaten, it becomes a part of the one who consumes it. The bride of Christ is being commissioned to go once again to the nations of the earth and demonstrate the reality of the gospel of the Kingdom. On the horizon is a prophetic proclamation concerning many nations, tongues, tribes, and kings; these will unfold the Kingdom to our generation.

As the Lord came to earth with the open book in His hand, John heard seven peals of thunder as He placed His foot on the land and sea. Each thunder crack had its own discernible voice. Something strategic and mysterious was articulated at the sound of that thunder, but it has remained a mystery because John was not permitted to write what he heard.

It will now be the responsibility of the bride of Christ to ask Heaven to reveal these profound mysteries and release them on earth as part of our end-time mandate. Heaven's blueprint has the fullness of redemption unveiled by the body of people to which the Head has been joined.

Initially John wept when he saw the book sealed with seven seals (Revelation 5:4) containing the mysteries of the Kingdom. But now the only One worthy to open the seals has come to earth to unveil the mysteries and strategies of the Kingdom through His holy ones. The Lord's present call to His covenant people is to begin to access that open book (scroll) and consume the revelation of Jesus. We must become a living expression of it. This revelation is the hidden manna set apart behind the veil of the Holy of Holies for the "victorious ones" who partake in the attributes and rewards of those who overcome.

*The Lord's present call to His covenant people is to begin to access that open book (scroll) and consume the revelation of Jesus.*

The bride is being commissioned to prophesy concerning many peoples, nations, tongues, and kings (Revelation 10:11) and demonstrate the maturation of the Kingdom message to the peoples of the earth. John, in Revelation 10, represents an end-time company of people to whom these mysteries will be delegated. These are consecrated believers who have found favor in the Lord's sight and allowed Him to purge, purify, and cleanse them spirit, soul, and body. Their sole desire will be to embody the living Word and steward Heaven's agenda and Christ's motives.

The spirit of wisdom and revelation will rest upon this body and bring understanding of the Kingdom's mysteries and the great and mighty things we have previously not known.

Both Daniel and John saw weighty end-time purposes but were instructed to seal up what they saw until the time of the end. Since the restoration of the Jewish people to their Promised Land, we are living in those days. The prophetic time clock is ticking.

The Holy Spirit, through Paul, outlines this great mystery:

Eye has not seen, nor ear heard,
Nor have entered into the heart of man
The things which God has prepared for those who
    love Him.
But God has revealed them to us through His Spirit.
For the Spirit searches all things, yes, the deep things
    of God.
                              —1 Corinthians 2:9–10, NKJV
                              (quoting Isaiah 64:4; 65:17)

Awesome things, hidden in God until now, are being unveiled by the spirit of revelation, according to Paul. In his letter to the Ephesians, he revealed a key secret concerning the mysteries of Heaven—they are hidden in Christ (Ephesians 3:9; Colossians 3:3–4). It was necessary for these great strategies of Heaven to be concealed because of the human tendency to corrupt what God releases to us. God will administer, govern, and make known the mysteries and unfathomable riches harbored in His heart. Conversely, the enemy's plan is to counterfeit every genuine expression from Heaven that he is capable of duplicating, corrupting, perverting, or twisting.

On the day Jesus fed the five thousand with just a few morsels of bread and fish, He used His disciples' hands to multiply and distribute the food. Paralleling this natural activity, trustworthy stewards of Kingdom mysteries and power will emerge to delegate the revelation of the open book, thereby multiplying and distributing spiritual sustenance. The Lord will bless this bread and break it so that desperately hungry souls can discover the unveiling of His Kingdom and experience, firsthand, the King.

CHAPTER

# 11

# GOD'S SECRETS

Today's believers should be encouraged by the Bible's promise that the Kingdom of God will be demonstrated in these last days. Heaven's strategy, foreseen by the prophets and foretold in Scripture, contains candid and profound prophetic promises. Several generations of prophets and seers used their revelatory gifting to forecast a day where God's promise would fully manifest in a body of consecrated people.

"To those who overcome" is a noteworthy identification that directs the destiny of a unique group of people. Throughout the Judeo-Christian ages, those who have overcome spiritual adversity have been rewarded with Kingdom blessings and though the enemy may try and counterfeit God's genuine expression, those who overcome are ultimately victorious in their struggle with the demonic hordes.

This incredibly important issue of overcoming is not as

salient as one might think. There is a way that seems right to a person, but the end thereof is destruction. Jesus clearly warned in Matthew 24 that a form of religion would emerge that is so close to authentic godliness that, if possible, it will deceive the very elect. This subtle form of deception can be linked to the fifth "I will" of Satan and his evil desire to be "like the Most High" (Isaiah 14:13–14). He attempts to produce a form of religion that fulfills his hunger to steal the abundant life God promised His people (2 Timothy 3:5).

In every expression of revival and spiritual outpouring throughout Church history, the enemy has used zealous religious activity and natural beauty to corrupt human beings. However, in the new day that has arrived the overcomers will finally attain their rewards. This victorious company will recognize the enemy's misleading attempts to steal the birthrights of God's people.

In Revelation John recorded the rewards awaiting the victorious company identified in each of the seven churches of Asia. These rewards represent Christ's heritage delegated to His bride. One gift that has always been of particular significance to me personally is the promise made to the "overcomers" of the Pergamum church. The Lord promises them He will:

". . . give some of the hidden manna, and I will give him a white stone, and a new name written on the stone which no one knows but he who receives it."
—Revelation 2:17

Receiving a new name and partaking of hidden nourishment seem intriguing and inviting. These mysteries are hidden from the wise and intelligent but freely revealed to babes, to the Lord's friends, attests John 15:15.

There are several instances in Scripture where God gave a man or woman a new name. This name change was always accompanied by a character change and an impartation of heavenly virtue for a specific task. Revelation 2:17 adds another layer to that: The "hidden manna" is set apart and reserved for the spiritual nourishment of a body of people willing to access this privilege.

One of the great revelations to emerge in this generation is the qualification to be identified as an "overcomer." Since Pentecost, a message of truth has been given to each of the Church ages. It has been the bread of life for that generation, a word from the spirit of truth that had to be embraced and experienced.

In Martin Luther's day, the manna was the message of justification by faith. This fresh and unprecedented truth countered the religious structure of the day that mandated association with an institution rather than with the Savior.

> *The "hidden manna" is set apart and reserved for the spiritual nourishment of a body of people willing to access this privilege.*

After that generation John Wesley, George Whitefield, and many others brought forth a message of sanctification. This was another heavenly release of manna in the progressive restoration of the birthright of the Church.

The beginning of the twentieth century witnessed the restoration of the *charismata*, with the gifts of the Spirit, speaking in tongues, and the experience of the "in-filling." This started at Azusa Street and has spread around the world.

Each generation has been given heavenly manna, with God rewarding those who overcame the religious structures of their day to embrace that deposit of truth. The seven letters to the churches of Asia include some of these invitations. Those seven messages depicted a clear spiritual appreciation of the past two thousand years of Church history, along with applicable correction, encouragement, and admonition.

The instruction and promise to the Laodicean church embodies unique application and prominence for this generation. It is a clear prophetic directive offered to the twenty-first-century Church and lays out one of the most compelling rewards conferred to any generation of overcomers. The victorious ones are given the unthinkable privilege of being seated with Christ on His throne, just as He overcame to sit with the Father.

A direct link exists between the Revelation 4:1 invitation and the message to the Laodicean church (Revelation 3:14–22). The overcoming body is positionally and experientially seated on the Lord's throne; that group is then invited to experience throne room revelation.

## An Invitation to the Throne

During the spring of 2001, I was involved in a conference with Bobby Connor and others in Abbotsford, British Columbia, Canada. What the Holy Spirit did during that time left me with a deep sense of faith and an assurance about the present invitation to approach God's throne and apprehend throne room visitations. It was as if God's Kingdom realm were being unveiled.

Before one of the evening services I was introduced to Mrs. Lorrie White, a precious woman who clearly carried considerable spiritual authority. She and her husband, Dr. John White, had faithfully served the Lord for half a century as missionaries and pioneers. John had written several important books, including an outstanding work called *When the Spirit Comes with Power* about John Wimber and the early days of the Vineyard movement.

After we entered the service, I and the rest of the leadership team took our seats in the front row. I noticed that Mrs. White took the seat directly behind me in the second row. That night Bobby Connor was speaking. Midway through his message Bobby left the podium and began to wander around the altar, prophesying to individuals whom the Holy Spirit was highlighting to him. Not surprisingly the Lord had Bobby bring Mrs. White to the front of the church, and he shared some prophetic insight with her. He called me forward and asked me to minister to her also, giving any prophetic direction the Lord offered. (Over the years I have learned to be spontaneous and prepared in season and out, especially when Bobby "conducts" the service!)

As I asked the Lord for prophetic revelation for Mrs. White, I could only offer a few words of encouragement and edification. At the end of this brief time of ministry I returned to my seat. The moment I sat down, though, the Lord spoke to me concerning Mrs. White.

> *"She is like Esther ... I have extended My scepter to her because I knew her request would be consistent with the desire of My heart."*

"She is like Esther . . . I have extended My scepter to her because I knew her request would be consistent with the desire of My heart."

*It would have been nice to know that while I was standing in front of a thousand people prophesying to her,* I thought to myself. Now I wondered how I was going to share this very specific word I felt was quite significant.

As Bobby returned to the podium he turned to me a second time and motioned for me to join him. He asked if I had any additional prophetic insight to share with the Body. I knew this was my opportunity. I shared the Esther revelation with

Mrs. White and the congregation as I had heard it from the Holy Spirit. It seemed to have a deep impact; I had no idea how deep until much later.

Bobby and I prophetically ministered to a few other people and began to close the service. As we were about to finish I asked Mrs. White to join us and pronounce a blessing over the assembly. When she came forward, she asked if she might tell the congregation about a series of open visions that had recently been entrusted to her. I was staggered by what followed.

Mrs. White told us she had been given a series of three extraordinary visionary experiences. She said it was as if a television screen had been pulled down in front of her and she could see, with her open natural eyes, the unfolding of revelatory insight. That is the very definition of an "open vision."

In the first vision one Tuesday night, Mrs. White saw the Lord Jesus standing on a balcony. He was clapping His hands and excitedly calling His people forward to Himself.

The following morning a second vision came: She saw the Lord Jesus standing before His throne plainly holding His scepter of ultimate authority and virtue.

The third, and final, open vision occurred on Wednesday evening. This vision seemed to pick up where the last one left off. The Lord was still standing before His throne holding His scepter. However, this time he extended His scepter to the people who had responded to the invitation to come before His heavenly throne.

The Lord then said:

"I am holding the scepter out to you, but I will not touch you with it; you, My people, must come and touch it for yourselves. It carries My wisdom . . . My righteousness . . . My humility . . . My authority . . . My direction, and My anointing. It is not enough to say I am available—this is not the time to wait . . . this is the time to move forward toward Me. I am your direction for the future. I will never withdraw My scepter. It will remain—it is available and it holds all of who I am. It is now available to you, My Church."

Mrs. White followed up this incredible series of visions with a prophetic charge:

"The Captain of the Lord of Hosts has summoned us to the throne room to touch His scepter of wisdom, authority, provision, grace, and anointing. Jesus is coming again for His bride. He is indeed shaking the nations—make sure your feet are planted solidly in Him. Jesus is saying to the Church that He desires to meet her in the throne room to share the things He has to tell us. Do not say you are not sufficiently trained or that you have only had basic training. Beloved, we are never fully prepared for war. In this upcoming war you will gain your experience on active duty. We have been called up to receive our orders, directions, and provision from Headquarters. There are no options or refusals. The Lord of Hosts has called us to His throne room to touch His scepter. Will you?"

We were stunned at this affirmation of the prophetic word I had shared earlier. Mrs. White and I hadn't discussed an Esther impartation nor had she given any hint that she had encountered the Lord in this way. Only the Holy Spirit could have orchestrated this exchange with the impact it carried. For Bobby and I, as well as for others in the meeting, the way these events unfolded amplified the force of the message and high-lighted the incredible opportunity being given to the Church to encounter the Lord.

Those who overcome hear the Lord say "come up here." It is there, before His throne, that we apprehend His heart and discover His unfathomable riches. Unprecedented opportunities are being offered to those who desperately press in to the Lord to obtain favor and help from the throne of grace. These will be the champions of the Lord who are seated with Him on His throne.

### Seated with Christ

Being seated with Christ in heavenly places signifies the delegation of authority. The process of redemption gives us a divine opportunity to share in the Kingdom rule of the Lord and to be entrusted with a realm of authority signified by the "seat" of dominion. Certainly, that designation is not randomly given; it is not simply handed out to every infant in the faith. While the position can be in no way earned or merited, it does evidence growth and maturity polished by the tutorial work of the Holy Spirit. This process molds us into the image of Christ, enabling us to maintain this spiritual position without corrupting or prostituting its sacred spiritual value.

*According to the admonition Jesus gave to the Laodicean church, those who overcome are granted permission to sit with Him on His throne, just as He overcame to sit with the Father.*

According to the admonition Jesus gave to the Laodicean church, those who overcome are granted permission to sit with Him on His throne, just as He overcame to sit with the Father.

A process of triumph over spiritual deception and resistance must be attained in order to qualify for this lofty office. Yielding to the work of grace positions the bride to share in her Bridegroom's nature and qualify for this heavenly position.

This is not a position we flippantly approach merely by walking down the aisle of a church and reciting a prayer. It happens when individuals experientially encounter the Lord of glory and are transformed into His image. Out of this stance of union and fellowship, the overcomers are seated and granted authority to rule with Him.

What Satan could not obtain through pride and rebellion, the Lord freely offers us by virtue of His sacrificial offering and work of redemption.

We are presently living in the transition from the Laodicean church age into the manifestation of Kingdom reality. I believe a tremendous display of truth is coming as manna for this day. It will transform and prepare a body of people to engage the Kingdom of Heaven fully and manifest that reality on earth.

Even during the Dark Ages when the written word was inaccessible to the masses, the living Word (Jesus) manifested Himself to those who were genuinely seeking Him with a pure heart and right motives. Many historical accounts validate this reality.

Paul was privileged to present the bread of life to his generation. As a reward for that leadership and sacrifice he was accorded the honor of presenting the "overcomers" of his day to the Lord as a chaste virgin. He wrote:

I am jealous for you with a godly jealousy; for I betrothed you to one husband, so that to Christ I might present you as a pure virgin.

—2 Corinthians 11:2

That same privilege is given to the messengers from each generation charged with presenting the manna of their day to the rest of God's people. The distinguished honor of God's anointed governmental leaders will be to prepare and present a body of people as a chaste virgin to her Lord.

Messengers have been sent to every age with a divine mandate and deposit of truth. They have had a fire locked up in their bones that must be expressed and demonstrated. They are like stars in the hand of the Lord, ready to present the heavenly revelation to the Body of Christ. In order to groom a people to reflect Christ's likeness and nature, an unprecedented amount of heavenly manna through many messengers, will be released in this day. It will be a multiplication of the "light" shining throughout the seven Church ages. According to the prophecy of Isaiah:

> The light of the moon will be as the light of the sun,
> and the light of the sun will be seven times brighter
> like the light of seven days, on the day the LORD binds
> up the fracture of His people and heals the bruise He
> has inflicted.
>
> —Isaiah 30:26

The loyalty of Abraham's servant, Eleazar, typifies these messengers of God. Eleazar was sent with a message and gifts to secure a chaste virgin for Isaac, the heir of Abraham's promise. This future bride could not be any ordinary woman; she had to be of the same heritage and lineage as Isaac. She had to become bone of his bone and flesh of his flesh.

In this current day, "Eleazars" are emerging as loyal and faithful servants. They are trustworthy stewards of divine mysteries and power and have been sent to secure a radiant and passionate bride for the Lord.

Daniel was shown the great deposit of mysteries that would unfold in the days identified as the "end-time" but was not allowed to articulate that revelation. Rather, it was reserved by Heaven, along with the secrets John observed and was required to seal (Daniel 12:4; Revelation 10:4).

Manna is described in the Bible as the bread of angels. It was the heavenly provision for the wandering children of Israel. It was the perfect sustenance for them in the Sinai desert. While they ate this bread from Heaven no one was feeble or sick. The manna symbolized the Messiah, the very bread of Heaven who would come and provide all humanity needed spiritually.

Those who eat this bread shall live forever without illness or weakness. Jesus Himself told us that humans shall not live by physical bread alone but by every Word proceeding from the mouth of God. It is not an optional duty—the grace of God demands that we be identified with those who overcome and share in the blessings and rewards of His "victorious ones." The revelation of His *logos* and *rhema* Word is our bread from Heaven. It is the spiritually nutritious manna that will perfectly sustain us.

*It is not an optional duty—the grace of God demands that we be identified with those who overcome and share in the blessings and rewards of His "victorious ones."*

Throughout Israel's history and in each Church age a portion of heavenly manna was given. The early apostles were entrusted with great revelation and insight into Kingdom mysteries, and a segment of the people embraced that revelation. However, compromise entered the corporate body in A.D. 325 when an organizational spirit severed the free flow of manna from Heaven. Only small measures of the bread of life came for the fifteen hundred years that followed. When the Lord remembered the promises of Joel 2:25, He began the process of progressive restoration. This started with the Great Reformation.

We are standing on the threshold of the generation long foreseen by the prophets and patriarchs. The holy ones of this day will not only be granted access to the manna of Heaven but also will partake of the grace to apprehend this experiential reality. This will be the generation to whom the Lord comes by placing His foot on the land and the sea, clothed in a rainbow, and with the open book in His hand. For many generations the book (scroll) has been sealed, but the end-time body has the unimaginable promise of living in the day in which the Lord Himself will break all seven of its seals open. It is His promise to give the now-open book to His betrothed ones as hidden manna for a generation hungry to consume the reality of Heaven (Revelation 10).

**Blessing the Bread**
One of Jesus' great miracles was the multiplication of the fishes and loaves. This act gives us a prophetic picture of the Lord supernaturally providing bread for His hungry followers. The miraculous provision was then given to the disciples, who delivered it to the masses. The Lord took the bread and gave it a supernatural blessing; He multiplied it so that all who were hungry had more than enough. The Lord will always make a way to provide bread for those who are hungry for it.

The prophet Daniel once made a statement for the ages: "There is a God in Heaven who reveals mysteries" (Daniel 2:28). That profound declaration is as true today as on the day it was spoken.

The Lord gives His victorious ones access to His mysteries when they overcome the religious structure of their day. This religious spirit is represented as clouds without water that merely rely upon intellectual and psychological reasoning (Jude 11-14). It steals faith and denies the supernatural dimension of God.

Human strength and reasoning simply will not be enough to fulfill end-time mandates. The wisdom and revelation we desperately need rests only in the Lord's heart. As Daniel expressed:

> This mystery has not been revealed to me for any wisdom residing in me more than in any other living man, but for the purpose of making the interpretation known to the king, and that you may understand the thoughts of your mind.
>
> —Daniel 2:30

Entrance to this realm is gained through God's power and revelation, which transcends the natural world. The Lord desires to open His treasuries to those who embrace every word that proceeds from His mouth.

## Manna Behind the Veil

As Moses was commanded to place three-and-a-half pints of manna in the Ark of the Covenant (Exodus 16:32–33), so also has a portion of heavenly manna been set apart and reserved behind the heavenly veil. In the Old Testament the high priests would go behind the veil after following the careful prescription of Heaven for entrance to the Holy of Holies. Aaron and the subsequent high priests were allowed entrance to the Holiest Place to discover the manifest presence of God and the sacred elements ordained by God to be kept there. From there they delegated the revelation they received to their generation.

In like manner the royal priesthood is granted access to the very throne of Heaven, where hidden manna and the mysteries of the ages are held and reserved in God's heart. The Spirit searches all things, even the depths of God, where His thoughts and ways are accessed.

When the bride of Christ embraces the treasure of knowledge and wisdom from behind the veil, she will be without spot or wrinkle. These secrets are the fruit of intimate relationship and affectionate communion with the Lord. Intimacy is His deepest desire.

### The Revelation of Jesus Christ

The hidden manna is none other than the revelation of Jesus Christ. The book of Revelation is the *apocalypse,* a term from Greek meaning "uncovering"—the unveiling, manifestation, and divinely granted appearance of the Lord Jesus Christ. When we eat the open book (scroll), it becomes a part of us and we become a part of Him. It is not sufficient simply to look at the open book or hear expressions from it; we must consume it to satisfy our spirit's hunger for the revelation of who He is.

It will take all of eternity to apprehend fully the vastness of His nature and character, but we are introduced to that lofty place on this side of eternity by the ones who overcome. This is the mystery of discovering the hope of His calling, the riches of the glory of His inheritance in the saints, and the surpassing greatness of His power toward those who believe (Ephesians 1:18–19). The Lord Himself will delegate the manna of Heaven and the bread of life to satisfy the many questions, yearnings, and aspirations of His people.

As a blessing, the overcomers not only receive access to the hidden manna but also a white stone with a new name written upon it. No one knows that new name except those who receive it. It is part of the change of nature and character imparted to those who are victorious in this battle and share in this blessed promise. Abraham, Sarah, Jacob, Peter, and Paul all illustrate this reality with the changing of their names to reflect the transference of their natures from earthly to heavenly. After a name changes, promises are given.

Jacob wrestled with God; that heavenly encounter marked a point in his life when he began to be recognized as a prince before God and humanity.

On the day of Pentecost, the Church was born, as anointed men and women fully yielded themselves to the Holy Spirit and began to comprehend the great mysteries of the Kingdom. So shall it be at the consummation of the ages—but in a multiplied fashion. The days following Pentecost were only a new stage and birthing. The upcoming stage will see the fullness of the mysteries unfolded through vessels of our generation consumed with God and fully submitted to His plan and purpose.

## Prophetic Glimpses of This Day

Over the past century there have been several prominent leaders who greatly impacted their generations with the demonstration of the Spirit and His power. They seemed to transcend their generations and apprehend promises that would characterize the last of the latter days. They became representative of the Kingdom people who will constitute the great army depicted in the prophecies of Joel. In many ways they were prototypes of the overcoming Body that will receive the blessings of the "victorious ones."

Maria Woodworth-Etter is one of the saints who provide a prophetic model for Kingdom ministry. She was a spiritual pioneer and forerunner who blazed a trail in the Spirit for others to follow. Mighty miracles and healings characterized her meetings, along with other expressions of Heaven's revelatory realm as visions and trances were also commonplace in her ministry.

On March 24, 1904, Woodworth-Etter was taken in a trance to witness prophetically attributes of the Body of Christ's last days and how the Lord will deal with His people before His imminent return. In the experience she first observed the Lord on the cross, drawing His people to Himself. This seemed to portray how a deep revelation of the cross will profoundly equip this company. She then saw many believers' desperate desire to apprehend the reality of heavenly experiences. She noted that the higher each individual went, the more brightly he or she was illuminated in the Spirit. She understood that we are the light of the world and that our lamps are lit in Heaven. The higher we ascend in the Spirit, the more brilliantly our light is displayed.

> It was as if the finger of God were placed upon the foreheads of those who are sealed in Christ and imparted supernatural comprehension of His Word and Kingdom mysteries.

She was also shown the great darkness that will permeate the latter days. The Lord told her that many are called to display His overcoming victory in this generation, but very few will be chosen or will choose to accept this divine invitation. She was shown the heavenly preparation required for this to happen. The Lord was gathering His hosts (armies), preparing spiritual horses and chariots to carry heavenly virtue to His people. She saw a great spiritual awakening in the very last days as well.

In another vision of the last days she saw the Father's hand descending from Heaven and touching His people with His love. It was as if the finger of God were placed upon the foreheads of those who are sealed in Christ and imparted supernatural comprehension of His Word and Kingdom mysteries. During the experience she was told that many would be supernaturally gifted with the spirit of wisdom and given a special knowledge of the glorious divine plan for the ages. And in the proper season, spiritual meat would be furnished by Heaven to prepare the bride of Christ for Jesus' return. Most importantly Maria Woodworth-Etter witnessed how the love of God would permeate the army of overcomers dedicated to presenting God's Kingdom on earth. This company is called to reveal the abundant inheritance resident in Christ and expressed in His word.

Scripture, and the mysteries contained therein, does not originate by human will. It comes when the Holy Spirit moves upon men and women speaking from God (2 Peter 1: 21).

Revelatory knowledge combined with experiential reality equals divine wisdom. We embody God's wisdom when our understanding of Scripture is consolidated with supernatural encounters with the Holy Spirit to bring a living reality to the expression of God's Word.

The Lord's awesome thoughts and ways are not able to be interpreted through human reasoning or natural wisdom but by the divine revelation of Jesus Christ. As Paul wrote:

> For this reason I, Paul, the prisoner of Christ Jesus for the sake of you Gentiles—if indeed you have heard of the stewardship of God's grace which was given to me for you; that by revelation there was made known to me the mystery, as I wrote before in brief.
>
> —Ephesians 3:1–3

Affectionate, genuine adoration and praise to God will follow the declaration and embracing of the bread of Heaven (Daniel 2:47).

Paul was a carrier of God's heart; he considered it his duty and privilege to access the hidden manna from behind the veil and impart it to the people of his day. He was also privileged to be able to write His revelation plainly so that we who read it with spirit eyes could understand it. Like the high priests of old, Paul was allowed into the Holy of Holies and permitted to share in the hidden manna, the bread of life. His oral and written proclamations continue to earn fruit unto eternal life that is credited to his heavenly account. Likewise, those who make known the manna for this day will reap immeasurable dividends in eternity.

There are devoted believers called to access and delegate hidden manna in this generation. The commission of this royal priesthood is to make known God's mysteries and secrets and to discover and proclaim Heaven's plans and purposes that were orchestrated before the foundation of the world. Though God's design is hidden from the world, it is freely bestowed on His covenant people—both old and new, who are one in Messiah—and expressed through the spirit of revelation.

According to His good pleasure and merciful intent, the Lord Jesus intends to unify all things under His headship at the climax of the ages, consummating all the prophecy throughout history by means of consecrated people joined to Him. This is the bread of life and hidden manna for our day.

An age-old mystery is now being manifested and revealed to a holy body of people: The full expression and experiential apprehension of Jesus Christ residing within—Christ in us, the hope of glory. From this company an army of champions will arise to demonstrate the Kingdom like no generation before it.

# chapter 12

# THE EMERGENCE *of* SPIRITUAL CHAMPIONS

As someone once said, "Life is like a library owned by an author. In it are a few books which he wrote himself, but most of them were written for him." Recorded in the annals of history are many tales about warriors and conquerors that provide valuable lessons about becoming a spiritual champion. The United States has always extolled sports heroes and their accomplishments, and celebrities, as well as ordinary people who have done extraordinary things. I have always been encouraged by studying the accounts of strength, determination, perseverance, and willingness to take risks of those who excel at and become the best at what they do.

Great champions of God will blossom in this day doing exploits for His glory. We can learn a great deal by exploring and analyzing both spiritual and secular figures who are considered emblems of courage, determination, and victory.

Several years ago the United States witnessed one of the most uncommon accounts of a great champion in history. This victor's life story is filled with symbolic meaning and life applications for this generation of purpose and destiny.

My first exposure to this luminary were broadcasts by nationally recognized sports announcers, who described him as a "godsend" and advised listeners that "to watch him run was like a supernatural event." As the announcers spoke mystically and reverentially I wondered who such an awesome hero could be. To my surprise it was not a man or woman but a horse named Secretariat.

### Secretariat

In 1973 Secretariat rose out of obscurity to become recognized as one of the greatest racing horses in history. At that time interest in horse racing was at an all-time low in the United States, but this exceptional horse changed all that. Because of Secretariat's prior history, no one thought he had much of a chance at the Kentucky Derby. Experts believed that the race's distance or field offered little chance for a record-setting performance. Yet, to the surprise of everyone, Secretariat ran the first quarter-mile of this prestigious race in slightly more than twenty-five seconds, setting a new world-record pace. But could such a large and broad-shouldered horse maintain that stride and pace for another mile? Everyone wondered.

> *...to the surprise of everyone, Secretariat ran the first quarter-mile of this prestigious race in slightly more than twenty-five seconds, setting a new world-record pace.*

Surprisingly, Secretariat did better than just sustain that pace. He increased it with each quarter of the race, finishing

the one-and-a-quarter mile distance in less than two minutes—
an achievement unmatched before or since.

Suddenly a media frenzy began to flourish around this beau-
tiful red horse. Observers described him as "truly magnificent."
He graced the covers of *Time*, *Newsweek*, and *Sports Illustrated*.
A champion had been born!

## The Preakness

Excitement began to build as the Preakness, the second race in
the coveted Triple Crown, approached. The nation's attention
was turned to this beautiful horse, about whose attributes
commentators struggled to find appropriate adjectives. One
announcer claimed that in human vernacular Secretariat
would be a Heisman Trophy winner, a Rhodes Scholar, and
Miss America all in one stunning, awe-inspiring being.

In a unique way Secretariat's performance at the
Preakness was even more brilliant than his victory at the
Kentucky Derby. Secretariat was in last position out of the
starting gate but still did something unprecedented in this
historic race: He sprinted full-bore around the first bend, and
by the time he turned onto the back side, he was racing to the
lead. Now, the turns on this track are tight, and horse-racing
aficionados considered it suicidal to take the first bend too
fast. Nevertheless, Secretariat did the extraordinary in his second of three monumental races. Veteran racing experts were
awestruck, declaring, "Horses don't do what he did here
today. They just don't do that!"

As he had at the Kentucky Derby, Secretariat won the
Preakness by two-and-a-half lengths. Many believe the pace of
this race was also record-setting, but because of a controversy
over the time clock, the speed was never verified.

With two victories under his belt all that stood between

Secretariat and the Triple Crown was the Belmont Stakes. One journalist said that if Secretariat were to lose the Belmont, "the country may turn sullen and mutinous." World attention was focused on this single race, which some would later describe as "the greatest race ever run."

**The Greatest Race**
On the morning of the Belmont Stakes Secretariat awoke with a seemingly mystical determination. His trainers later told reporters that he was "rearing and bucking, flaring his nostrils and rolling his eyes." He was somehow filled with anticipation for the race. Reportedly "he burst from the barn like a stud-horse going to the breeding shed and walked around the outdoor ring on his hind legs, pawing at the sky in a magical, unforgettable instant, now frozen in time."

Secretariat totally intimidated his competition approaching the starting gate; a supernatural atmosphere appeared to surround him. He did not merely walk to the gate—he romped to his position.

The Belmont was the longest of the three races. After the starter's gun had sounded, initially a horse named Sham gave Secretariat a formidable challenge. The first six furlongs were run in a staggering seventy seconds, with Sham incredibly keeping abreast of Secretariat. However, the pace proved more than Sham could sustain, and the challenger injured himself in the last race he would ever run.

Meanwhile, Secretariat continued to command the lead during the second half of the race. As one commentator put it, "It was as though he were running on the wind." Midway through the race it was clear Secretariat would win the Belmont and become the first new Triple Crown winner in twenty-five years. Yet, even more astonishingly, instead of coasting to a safe victory, Secretariat maintained the same record-setting pace; he did not merely want to win—he intended to run the greatest race ever.

Certain no horse could maintain this pace for so long, many observers and journalists felt jockey Ron Turcotte was foolish to continue to push Secretariat at this tempo and risk collapse and the loss of the Triple Crown victory. But the jockey had little to do with it: Secretariat was running at his own pleasure. This was a day of destiny. Turcotte later commented that Secretariat had a mind of his own for this race, and he [Turcotte] simply held on and enjoyed the ride.

*As the last quarter of the race lay before Secretariat, every fan, journalist, and observer grew mesmerized by the fortitude and sheer talent of this amazing horse, whose victory turned out to be one of the greatest events in sports history.*

As the last quarter of the race lay before Secretariat, every fan, journalist, and observer grew mesmerized by the fortitude and sheer talent of this amazing horse, whose victory turned out to be one of the greatest events in sports history. His Triple Crown performance is unmatched in U.S. horse-racing history. It was the greatest single performance he had ever witnessed in a sporting event, recalls legendary golf champion Jack Nicklaus. When this mythic race was over, Secretariat had defeated his closest competition by thirty-one lengths and set an all-time record of 2:24, a feat previously considered impossible.

## The Secret of Secretariat's Success

What a great champion God created for us to learn from! Secretariat had a secret, which was only discovered at his death.

During an autopsy, medical examiners found that Secretariat had a perfectly healthy heart that was almost two-and-a-half times larger than an average horse's heart. Secretariat's heart weighed a staggering twenty-two pounds, whereas an average horse's heart weighs about eight-and-a-half pounds.

Secretariat had been given a supernatural heart. Almighty God, the Creator, had given this horse a special endowment and greater capacity than any other race-horse in recorded history.

When I asked the Lord why he gave Secretariat such a large heart, he replied quickly and concisely: "Because it pleased Me to do so." No matter what veterinarians' conjecture or animal-biologists' suppositions might attest, God had simply decided to create a great champion. As Isaiah 42:5-6 declares:

Thus says God the LORD,
Who created the heavens and stretched them out,
Who spread out the earth and its offspring,
Who gives breath to the people on it
And spirit to those who walk in it,
I am the LORD, I have called You in righteousness,
I will also hold You by the hand and watch over you,
And I will appoint You as a covenant to the people,
As a light to the nations . . .

So in this generation of prophetic destiny, at a unique time in human history, the Lord Jesus will demonstrate divine power and Kingdom virtue through obscure champions with "supernatural hearts." These champions' hearts will be enlarged with passion and desire for the Redeemer and with Heaven's compassion, which they will be able to transmit to a needy generation. Many, like Secretariat, will arise from obscurity to run some of the greatest races ever run.

## Isaiah 22:22

In a prophetically symbolic way, Secretariat's twenty-two pound heart could represent the generation soon to emerge with a commissioning from Isaiah 22:22:

> Then I will set the key of the house of David
>     on his shoulder,
> When he opens no one will shut,
> When he shuts no one will open.

The key to the house of David signifies a governmental people who, like King David, will be anointed as both worshipers and warriors. David is regarded in Scripture as a man after God's own heart. He possessed a special capacity in his heart for God and His Kingdom revelation. So shall the emerging generation of radical worshippers and warriors, who in a day unprecedented in history will champion fresh standards of excellence and victory.

David's heart prophetically portrays the nature of the champions of the Lord's army. They are dreaded by the forces of darkness, who will recognize Christ's victory that they convey. As the Psalmist recorded:

> Once you spoke in vision to Your godly ones,
> And said, "I have given help to one who is mighty;
> I have exalted one chosen from the people.
> I have found David My servant;
> With My holy oil I have anointed him."
> —Psalm 89:19-20

God gave David the power to become a champion of Israel. He exalted David as a hero chosen from among His people and anointed him with holy oil. David, foreseen and identified by the prophetic voice of his day, was truly a champion of Israel.

Forerunners and prototypes have championed God's purposes in the past, but today God is grooming an entire group of people to display His godliness. God desires to be made flesh through a body of people who are joined with Him in a holy consummation. As we live not by natural bread alone but by the living Word proceeding from the mouth of God—the Bread of Abundant Life—hidden truth of godliness will become part of our spiritual DNA.

Eye has not seen and ear has not heard, nor has it even entered into the human heart, those things which the Lord desires to reveal to His people—the great blueprint of Heaven. Mysteries that have been reserved deep in the Father's heart, locked away in the mind of Christ, and dispersed by the Holy Spirit who searches the deep things of God, await the passionate embrace of a latter-day company of overcoming, holy, victorious ones. Abba, His Spirit, and the Bridegroom say, "Come."

# ABOUT *the* AUTHOR

Paul Keith Davis spent twenty years in business before entering full-time ministry. He and his wife, Wanda, founded WhiteDove Ministries after the Lord sovereignly sent a beautiful white dove to them as a prophetic sign of their calling.

In recent years Paul Keith and Wanda have traveled extensively, speaking at conferences and churches and imparting the end-time mandate of preparing the Body of Christ for the glory and manifest presence of God.

Paul Keith has written two books—*The Thrones of Our Souls* and *Engaging the Revelatory Realm of Heaven*—as well as numerous articles for various Christian publications, including *Charisma* magazine, *AWE* magazine, and *MorningStar Journal*. For the past several years he has also cowritten *The Shepherd's Rod* with Bob Jones, a publication providing spiritual insight to the Church.

Paul Keith and Wanda reside in Orange Beach, Alabama. They have five children and four grandchildren.

**Thrones of Our Soul**
By Paul Keith Davis

With great spiritual insight, Paul Keith Davis
explains how the Lord deals with the sacred places
within our hearts that keep us from achieving
our prophetic destiny.
**Retail: $12**

Available online at www.streamsministries.com
Or by calling 1-888-441-8080

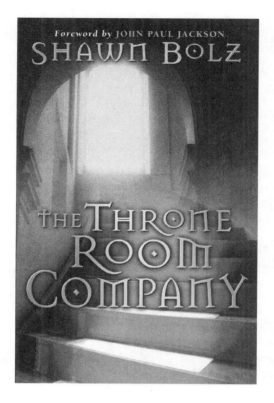

**The Throne Room Company**
By Shawn Bolz

Thought provoking and profoundly perceptive,
*The Throne Room Company* has the power
to revolutionize your understanding of God. In this
book, Shawn Bolz reveals a fascinating message
from heaven that will penetrate the deep places of
your heart. His stories and wisdom will guide you
to a more noble place.
**Retail: $12**

Available online at www.streamsministries.com
Or by calling 1-888-441-8080

## AWE Magazine

*AWE* seeks to inspire and empower people in
their quest for a spiritually fulfilling life.
You'll love *AWE*, including how it looks.
Each issue is visually attractive, making *AWE*
a treat for the eyes!

Subscribe now to *AWE*! Save up to 38%.
Call toll-free **1-888-441-8080**.
1 year (4 issues) for only $14.95  (U.S. only)
*(Foreign subscriptions, please add $10 delivery)*

**Naturally Supernatural**
By John Paul Jackson

A unique, unedited version of a workshop that took
place in Southampton, England, when John Paul
Jackson chronicled several exciting, supernatural
events. You'll hear hundreds of people squeal with
delight as nearly two dozen heavenly hosts become
visible to the eye, and fly through the room.
Many there were changed forever.
(Single CD)
**Retail: $9**

Available online at www.streamsministries.com
Or by calling 1-888-441-8080

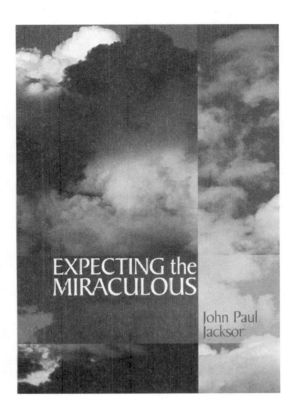

**Expecting the Miraculous**
By John Paul Jackson

Revolutionize the way you think about impossible
and overwhelming situations. In this inspiring
series, John Paul Jackson reveals how to take
difficult situations and transform them into
supernatural adventures. You'll discover how to
change your perceptions and what it means
to be empowered by faith.
(3-CD set)
**Retail: $22**

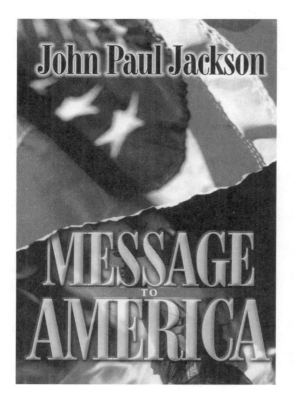

**Message to America**
By John Paul Jackson

On September 11, America was brought to its knees.
As Americans seek a path toward healing and
recovery, John Paul Jackson explains the proper
response to the dark events surrounding the
terrorist attacks on America and heaven's strategies
for the turbulent times ahead.
(Single CD)
**Retail: $9**

Available online at www.streamsministries.com
Or by calling 1-888-441-8080

**Preparing for Your Visitation**
By John Paul Jackson

Encounter God's transforming power in your life
like never before. In this life-changing series, John
Paul Jackson uncovers the greatest ploys of the
enemy that have hindered many from truley entering
into God's glorious presence. As you embrace these
truths, you will discover how to prepare for a
supernatural visitation from God.
(3-CD set)
**Retail: $22**

Available online at www.streamsministries.com
Or by calling 1-888-441-8080

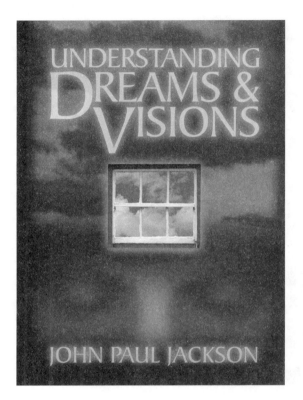

**Understanding Dreams and Visions**
By John Paul Jackson

Explore the world of dreams. Unravel the mysteries
of dream interpretation in this inspiring series and
discover how to apply God-given insights in your
waking life. You don't want to miss these fascinating
insights from a gifted dream expert.
(6-CD set)
**Retail: $42**

Available online at www.streamsministries.com
Or by calling 1-888-441-8080

**Moments with God Dream Journal**
By John Paul Jackson

John Paul Jackson shares his unique approach to dream recording and offers important keys to unearthing rewarding spiritual insights into your nightly adventures with God. Included in this journal is an introduction to dream journaling, three color wheels, sample journal entries, and specially designed forms to record your dreams and begin your own dream vocabulary.
Hardback
**Retail: $24**

**Needless Casualties of War**
By John Paul Jackson

Unlock the secrets of effective spiritual warfare.
Discover foundational truths that will help you
fight with wisdom and authority. John Paul Jackson
offers a theology of spiritual wafare that is simple,
yet so profound. Foreword by John Sandford.
**Retail: $13**

Available online at www.streamsministries.com
Or by calling 1-888-441-8080

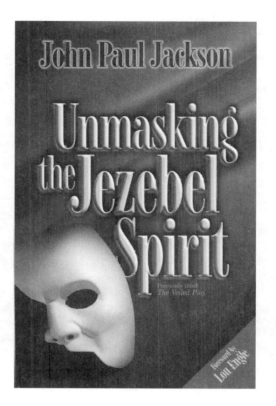

**Unmasking the Jezebel Spirit**
By John Paul Jackson

With keen insight, John Paul Jackson peers through
the enemy's smoke screen and exposes one of the
most deceptive snares used to destroy the Church.
Biblically anchored, this fascinating book is
seasoned with years of personal observation,
divine revelation, and thoughtful reflection.
Foreword by Lou Engle.
**Retail: $13**

Available online at www.streamsministries.com
Or by calling 1-888-441-8080

### Breath of I AM CD
By Graham Ord

*Breath of I AM* contains Graham Ord's original instrumental soundtrack from the *I AM: 365 Names of God* CD. Ideal for times of meditation, prayer, and therapeutic healing, this soothing instrumental creates an atmosphere that will uplift your spirit and calm your soul.
**Retail: $16**

Available online at www.streamsministries.com
Or by calling 1-888-441-8080

**I AM: 365 Names of God CD**
By John Paul Jackson

At the request of many people, John Paul Jackson
has gone into a studio and read the names of
God from his book, *I AM: 365 Names of God*. Many
can feel the inherent blessing and increase of faith
that happens from hearing these names read
aloud. Don't miss this exciting CD
from Streams Music Group!
**Retail: $16**

Available online at www.streamsministries.com
Or by calling 1-888-441-8080

**I AM: Inheriting the Fullness of God's Names**
By John Paul Jackson

As the richly dowried children of God, we are heirs to
God's abundant resources and wealth. Today, as well as
throughout eternity, we can reap the amazing blessings
of greater influence, favor, and protection that come with
God's name. By the mere power of His name, all healing
springs forth, all provisions flow, and all authority is
conferred. As you embark on the glorious adventure of
knowing God, let Him show you the amazing mysteries
and wonders reserved for those who bear His name.
**Retail: $10**

Available online at www.streamsministries.com
Or by calling 1-888-441-8080

**I AM: 365 Names of God**
By John Paul Jackson

Designed for daily reading and meditation,
John Paul Jackson has collected 365 names of God
that will guide you into becoming a person who
consistently abides in God's presence. God's names
are a disclosure of God Himself. In His name,
there is peace, comfort, provision, healing,
and destiny. When you meditate on a name of God,
you will discover His transforming power.
Hardback
**Retail: $24**

Available online at www.streamsministries.com
Or by calling 1-888-441-8080

**Streams Institute for Spiritual Development**
John Paul Jackson, Founder

At Streams, we seek to give shape to ideas that educate, inform, and cause people to better understand and delight in God. We endeavor to enrich people's lives by satisfying their lifelong need to identify and use their God-given gifts. We seek to be used by God to heal, renew, and encourage pastors and church leaders.

**Courses offered include:**
Course 101: The Art of Hearing God
Course 102: Advanced Prophetic Ministry
Course 104: Preparing for Your Visitation
Course 201: Understanding Dreams and Visions
Course 202: Advanced Workshop in Dream Interpretation

More information is available online at
www.streamsministries.com
Or by calling 1-888-441-8080